John Rhodes Speck

How I got my education

With a few remarks on I'm slightly in love as I pass on

John Rhodes Speck

How I got my education
With a few remarks on I'm slightly in love as I pass on

ISBN/EAN: 9783337270780

Printed in Europe, USA, Canada, Australia, Japan

Cover: Foto ©Lupo / pixelio.de

More available books at **www.hansebooks.com**

MY BLUE RIDGE MOUNTAIN HOME.

How I Got My Education.

WITH A FEW REMARKS ON I'M SLIGHTLY IN
LOVE AS I PASS ON,

By "The Special Agent."

Jas. P. Harrison & Co., Printers,
Atlanta, Ga.

TO THE STUDENTS OF EMORY COLLEGE
THIS LITTLE VOLUME
IS AFFECTIONATELY DEDICATED
BY THE AUTHOR.

Contents.

CHAPTER I.
My Desire for an Education, Confronted with Much Opposition.. 17

CHAPTER II.
My First Big Trip From Home.. 31

CHAPTER III.
Student, Teacher, Farmer and Agent............................ 46

CHAPTER IV.
At College and On the Road.. 61

CHAPTER V.
My Trip to Virginia.. 75

CHAPTER VI.
On the Road.. 90

CHAPTER VII.
Lights and Shadows, or Contrasted Pictures.............. 108

CHAPTER VIII.
Finale.. 127

Preface.

At the request of many who have taken much interest in his education, strewing his otherwise thorny pathway with flowers, and not as a specimen of literature, does the author send forth this little volume, hoping that by the suggestions contained therein, some struggling youth may find words of encouragement as he endeavors to honestly work his way through college and secure, by his own efforts, an education.

If it contains much that would seem ridiculous in the eyes of the refined, literary world, please remember that it is not a treatise on Morals, Science or Philosophy; nor is it a specimen of the author's true character; but merely a few pages from the book of Human Nature, as he picked them up by the wayside while pressing his journey along the busy thoroughfare of this bustling, battling world.

The author has tried to give, as nearly as possible,

the incidents as they occurred in his experience as an agent; this being the means which he employed to attain his education.

How few know the resources which lie within their reach, and still fewer are they who have the courage to utilize those they do discover; and it is with a view of encouragement, and not to seem literary, that he humbly sends this otherwise useless little volume on its mission of love.

May it find its way into the hands of those only, who are in sympathy with the young men who, oppressed with poverty, wish to make true men of themselves, and have first to acquire the wherewithal to secure sufficient mental training to insure success.

Then you will be kind in judgment and charitable in criticism. Most truly yours,

"THE SPECIAL AGENT."

Emory College, Oxford, Ga.

CHAPTER I.

MY DESIRE FOR AN EDUCATION CONFRONTED WITH MUCH OPPOSITION.

"Well, Pauline, this is the last note I shall ever carry for Clarence; I have magnified his virtues, exonerated him from his accused errors, loved him for his courage, and especially for your sake; I have plead his cause before you with an honest heart; but to-day I no longer carry a stick to break my own head. Hereafter the United States mail will bring his notes to you or they will lie unread. After this, the sweet-toned words from my lips will not be messages from him, but the pleadings of my own cause, from a heart too full for utterance now, too deep to be fathomed at a single glance."

The youth set his bucket of water down under the June apple tree, gazed silently for a moment upon the unsympathetic ground, and then dared to glance up into the sweetest face that he had ever beheld.

Instead of receiving a rebuke in the shape of a frown, the maiden, with flushed cheek and sparkling eye, broke the silence with words soft and encouraging.

"Jack, you need not carry another note for Clarence; I have read all from him that I care to read; henceforth he and I are merely friends. I thank you for all you have done for me in his behalf."

"Then, Pauline, live or die, sink or swim, survive or perish, I shall be hopeful that success is mine."

The "brown-eyed maiden" smiled an answer of love upon the courageous knight that would beggar words for description. The two turned and walked together up the green sward from the spring toward the old mansion, he to his work behind the counter in the basement, she up-stairs to busy herself in the domestic affairs of her happy home; he to dream of early becoming the partner and son-in-law of his employer; she to muse on Clarence's surprise and her own delight at being the queen of her father's senior clerk.

To fully appreciate the little thread of love which will run through these pages, showing the fatal rock upon which many a youth has wrecked his little *barque*, let us go back a few pages in the history of the hero of this story.

In that great valley of Virginia known as the Shenandoah—close by the foot of a spur of the "Blue Ridge" called the Massanutten Mountain—stands a small but attractive country cottage. In front of the house runs a bright, sparkling mountain branch, wind-

How I Got My Education.

ing through cedars, witchhazels and willows, watering the green meadow which stretches to the north of the cottage. Just behind this humble but Christian abode the mountain slope begins its ascent, rising for more than a mile and looking over the beautiful valley which sleeps so peacefully between these mountain ranges, after the din and bustle of four years' strife has been hushed to silence.

The war is over; the smoke of battle has now departed; the bugle no longer calls father to meet the foe who have so often laid waste their beloved and happy home. But is the father rich? Can he now retire and rest from his labors, educate his children and enjoy the comforts of an easy and quiet life? No, no! Would it had been so! With two mules and a horse brought out of the late conflict, a large family depending upon his efforts, on a small farm, some parts of which were very rocky, there was required the earnest attention of father and older boys, leaving but little time for thought and literary enjoyment.

Day after day and month after month did the youth of that humble home plow and sow, reap and mow, in those hot June-bug days; and haul wood and shovel snow in those long, cold Virginian winters.

There is much in a good, earnest desire. But desire, backed by an honest intention, together with a true conviction of right, becomes at once a power which must evidently create action—and action is all that is worth anything in this world. A man's desire may be wholesome, his purposes good, his convictions strong, but without action all falls hopelessly to the ground.

The eldest of the four boys had a desire to flee from the rocks and roots and harvest fields, and wood-hauling in snow storms, and seek a place more congenial with his mental and physical make-up. This youth had the honest conviction that he was never intended for a farmer; he might have been cut out for one, but was mightily spoiled in the making. He wanted to be a clerk.

This anxious desire to mix and mingle with prints and lawns, bleached cotton and dress goods, hose and slippers, ruffles and bustles, hooks and eyes, hair pins and braids, starch and lace collars, twenty-button kids and corsets, led this youth, with father's permission, from the farm to the store.

A grand departure, this! I remember leaving one cold December evening, behind another boy, on horseback, with my clothes tied up in an old-fashioned oil-cloth bag, and arriving at the residence of my employer after a ride of about fifteen miles, at nine o'clock that cold winter December evening.

Old Squire Prestine was the gentleman who had offered me the position as clerk in one of his dry goods stores; and it was his daughter, Pauline Prestine, that proved to be the heroine in the little story about to be recited. She was no heroine to me at that time. My goddess was the mercantile business, and I bowed in humble reverence to every proposition made me by my new employer.

Next morning, the bargain being made, and quite a meagre salary agreed upon, I was informed by the old Squire that my services were needed at one of his branch stores about twenty miles distant; but that the horses were busy, and my only chance to get there would be to walk.

"Walk twenty miles?"

"Yes, sir!"

"With these heavy brogan boots on, filled with Hungarian tacks to keep them from wearing out? Walk twenty miles over this hard, frozen ground without any dinner?"

"That's the programme," said the Squire; and I saw in his countenance a kind of a "you-can-do-that-or-go-back-home" expression. Then I thought, "There's no royal road to learning" the mercantile business. But thank kind fortune, I had the grit to try it.

Leaving the little village of L——, just as the sun rose from behind the snow-capped mountain peaks— painting the white frost into a thousand sparkling gems, and the sharp mountain air making red the nose

How I Got My Education.

and ears of the out-door boy, the new clerk was seen moving off in the direction of his new home.

After a two hours' walk, coming suddenly upon an eminence in the road, the steeple of the old town clock, the glittering spires of the churches, and the blue smoke curling and intermingling with the tall houses and tree tops, revealed to the ravished eyes of the country boy the beautiful town of H——, situated in the very heart of the Shenandoah Valley. To a youth unaccustomed to the fascinating ways of the world, this was a grand treat!

"I'll take in the town," said I. "I've started out to make money and see the world, and I'll soon have plenty of filthy lucre. So I'll just call in at one of these stores and pick me out a nice hat, send in for it soon, and throw this old slouched hat away; clerks don't wear such hats as this anyway."

So on my arrival at Main street, I stepped into one of the large dry goods stores, and a clerk approached me and said:

"Vell, vot ish it?"

"I wish to look at a fashionable hat, if you please."

"Vell, you kin schist look ad him. Dot ish ein goot hoot, dot ish ein besser hoot, und dot ish ein bestes hoot."

"What do you ask for the price of this hat?"

"Ein doller und zeventy-five zents, und ids sheat ad haf de moneys."

"All right, sir; I'll take this one if you will lay it away until I come to town again."

Eef you pays me ver id, I lays 'im avay."

"But, sir, I haven't the change now."

"Vell, den you pays me dwenty vive zents ver my droubles. Eef you dond, I calls in der bolice und has you bud in der schail."

Then I thought, "You vas von vool mit vooten head," and I walked out mighty quick, and struck up the road for my new home, where they had no "vool" Jews to bother me with "dot kind of beeshniss."

About three o'clock that afternoon I arrived at my destination with the skin all rubbed off my heels, awfully hungry and tired, but anxious to enter upon the duties of the high position to which I had been called. Next morning I was initiated into the business of country clerk.

Well, perhaps some young fellows don't know what the character of a new country clerk's duties is. Well, for three months I fed chickens and turkeys, ducks and geese, pigs and calves, packed rags and feathers, eggs and wool, dried fruits and pole-cat skins, swept out the store and carried water, cut wood and made fires!

A grand and elevated calling this! "Who would be a farmer when such a distinguished business as this could be had? Not this chicken," thought I.

But the stone which the builders rejected soon became the head of the corner. It was but a short time until the boss sent for me to come back to this town of L——, his place of residence, where I became the senior clerk, the corresponding secretary, the chief-cook-and-bottle-washer, and above all, oh! must I say it, I blush to murmur the rest, the—the man— the m-a-n who—who w-a-s in love with—with his employer's daughter!

Yes, it was in the little town of L——, that Clarence Morton, Pauline Prestine and myself, played a little game that mighty nearly bursted up my hopes for an education.

Three years of my life at L—— glided by as quietly as the running of Niagara Falls—for you know that true love runs as smoothly as Niagara and as musically as a dozen tom cats on a house-top in a midwinter night. Those were days of knightly glory! Pauline and I met in the parlor by the soft light of the burning taper; on the front piazza, in the softer and dimmer glow of the evening starlight, and by the spring, under the June-apple tree, as the day died away into dreamy twilight. We found it convenient to attend church together; to go to camp-meetings, picnics and parties—often through deep snow—when the music of the sleigh-bells chimed in so musically with the song our happy hearts were singing.

Thus summer and winter, autumn and spring, were all one season to us. Soon we should be married and I should be one of the firm—happy socially, happy as a business man—happy alway!

Clarence Morton had been Pauline's first sweetheart, and attractive and graceful as he was, the new clerk was too much for him.

Clarence stuck out his shingle as a lawyer and pointed to his profession as his mistress. He had retired from the fight, leaving me the successful knight with Pauline. I stood cock of the walk. Clarence drank —that's what ruined him with the old folks and with Pauline too. I had the advantage of him there—I did not drink. Boys, never drink!

But in the midst of all this feast of joy and expected perfection of bliss, a "sudden change came over the spirit of my dreams"; I had been raised by loving, Christian parents, who, if they could not give me an education, had tried to impress early piety upon my young heart, and suddenly I felt that the world was offering me too much; that I was in danger of cheating myself out of my soul—in a word, I felt called upon to spend my time and talents in the ministry.

What! Must I sacrifice my business relations with the old Squire, and be a poor man the rest of my days with the words of the poet ringing in my ears ever and anon—

"No foot of land do I possess,
  No cottage in this wilderness?"

Above all, must I sacrifice the only woman in the world who loves me, and sever these sweet ties which bind us into such a bundle of concentrated bliss? "Aye, there's the rub—it doth make cowards of us all." I knew that to preach would require a long and tedious course in college, besides the time it would take to get ready financially for prosecuting my studies. Moreover, to leave Pauline was to lose her; for she had not promised to wait five or six years for me, and then be a preacher's wife. I knew if she did promise she would not wait. But these were my honest convictions, worked out by many an hour of anxious thought, and thank goodness for a spirit that prompts a man to do what he believes to be his duty, even in the face of all opposition, and at the sacrifice of the dearest and sweetest idol of his brightest fancies.

Finally, I summoned up courage enough to break the secret to Pauline. It was a sad time indeed; but not so sad as I had expected. I had thought to see her turn coldly and indifferently away from me and leave me to weep alone. But when I said:

"Pauline, my convictions, from a moral standpoint, require that our marriage be postponed for at least five years, and that these pleasant associations be frequently broken into by intervals of long absence; that my life be spent in the ministry, which will require much time and preparation for such a life-work!"

When I revealed to her these, my recent convictions, why, like all other good little women, she was true as steel, for the moment.

"Pauline, to leave you is to lose you, I know—I know it is! You will not wait; and how can I lose you, the hope of all my future happiness?"

I turned to leave the room with an over-burdened heart, but, laying her hand on my shoulder, she said:

"Jack, I will wait for you, and when you return, an educated man, I will, if possible, be prouder of you than now."

"How kind and true you are; I know you will wait!"

(Yes; they all wait—but it is till some other fellow comes along) and I said to myself as I left the room:

"What will Clarence be doing in all my absence?"

The cold chills ran down my spinal column till I could have spit out ice-cream just by drinking sweet milk.

Next morning when the old Squire came in the store, I said:

"Squire, I'm very sorry, but I am going to leave in a few days—hope you will not be inconvenienced in finding some one to fill my place."

"Where are you going?" inquired the Squire, with some surprise upon his countenance.

"Going to educate myself, and spend my life in another vocation."

"Oh, nonsense! You have education enough. I was just thinking of turning over the new store, up on the river, and giving you half the profits."

"That's a fine offer, Squire; but my convictions lead me into another channel of life and activity."

"What is your programme for the future," inquired the Squire.

"My life will be spent in the ministry, sir."

"Oh, if that's it, your conscience will soon be at ease; it's a mere momentary conviction, which will blow over in a little while."

"I guess not, Squire; I've fought it too long and too hard already to be deceived. My purposes are fixed. I leave next Tuesday."

"I am sorry, very sorry, my boy, but I haven't anything more to say."

When the next Tuesday evening's sun sank to rest behind the blue hills in the far west, I sat under the weeping willow at my mountain home with book in hand, studying a lesson to recite to my sister the next day. For the next few months I was under the pleasant tutoring of my sweet sister, whose early advantages had been better in literary culture, and who had acquired some proficiency as an educator in our immediate neighborhood. But many were the times I stole off to the little village of L—— on a Saturday evening to see Pauline, and talk over our future prospects, when I should become an educated man, and fill my mission in life as an itinerant Methodist preacher.

How hard were the pages of rhetoric and the problems of mathematics to a mind whose early training had been thus neglected! How frequent were the wishes to be back at the village of L——, or a partner in the new store on the river, instead of trying to get an education without money or other necessary advantages. But in the face of all opposition I said, "I will," and things *wilted*.

But to accomplish my purposes, what more must be sacrificed? I cannot board at home and attend college, or even a good high school. I must go to some place where I can work for a while, and attend college for a while, and thus work my way over the seeming impassable barriers which loomed up in my pathway from ignorance to a moderate degree of mental attainment.

Virginia is a grand old State; her colleges are good, her climate conducive to culture, but to the poor boy there are other places where success is more certain, and certainly more rapid; and, thank goodness, Georgia is such a place. While her sons were left poor from the ravages of the war, there is no place in the Southern States where there are finer facilities for young men to utilize in attaining education. Her winters are mild, giving more time in which to work; the people are kind and generous, often lending a helping hand to the toiling youth, as he seeks employment.

Teachers and canvassers, especially those who go out in the summer vacations from colleges, meet the approval of all true Georgians. It was to this field I was luckily directed, and will ever thank kind Providence for allowing my lines to fall in such pleasant places.

Of course to do this I must make one more final and exceedingly sad sacrifice—I must leave home! Write that sentence, will you, young man, and put it into action, and you will make the sacrifice that tells for good or for evil on the life of the youth, for time and for eternity. The holy influences of praying parents, the sweet association of loving sisters, and the heavenly benediction that hangs like an oracle about the parental roof, when once sacrificed, leaves an aching void that strangers' parents and other boys' sisters can never (fully) fill. The Paulines and the Susies, the Marys and the Janes may be found anywhere at any time, "the woods is full uv 'em," but mothers and fathers, sisters

How I Got My Education. 31

and brothers will be found nowhere in this broad world but at "*Home!*" But where they are, and there only, is home—whether in the fertile valley of the Shenandoah, or in the arid desert, or among the rocky cliffs of the Sierra Nevadas. For Heaven's sake, don't depreciate home. You may discount sweethearts fifty cents on the dollar, and then call it a good trade, but let home go for its par value, for "home is home, be it ever so homely."

CHAPTER II.

MY FIRST BIG TRIP FROM HOME.

IN the days of '76, when every railroad station was lined with the flaming advertisement, "Go West, Young Man, Go West!" and many of the noblest sons of the "Mother State" were taking up their march with the motley crowd, in their eager press across the Mississippi, some, perhaps, to fill the high calling of a "cow-boy," others to stump the State of Texas for the cause of temperance, with a bottle of whisky in each pocket, and others, doubtless, to be elected chief marshal at the lynching of some one of their own party, I heard a gentle voice, low, but sweet, saying, "Come to the 'land of the Sunny South,' a land whose genial sun, balmy air, fertile soil and generous people offer a rich harvest to those who "fear not to tread where duty leads.' "

This was a year for leaving home. Englishmen and Frenchmen left home that year, Germans and Scotchmen, Irishmen and Spaniards, Esquimaux and Laplanders, Icelanders and Portuguese, our Brother in Black, our Sister in Red, our Cousin John in Yellow, and our Uncle-connecting-link, the Baboon—all had left home that year and had congregated in Philadelphia at our "grand, gloomy and peculiar" Centennial.

It was indeed a time for leaving. New departures were taking place every day. So I began to pack.

First of all I must get rid of those things which I will not need when I get to Georgia, for Georgia, from a Virginia standpoint, has the finest climate in the world—a perfect fairy land—no rain except when and where it is absolutely needed, no mud, except at the brickyards, no snow nor ice nor cold weather, nor rocks, nor briars, nor thorns, nor thistles, nor snakes, nor mosquitoes, nor sandflies, nor "chiggers." No! nothing but flowers and fruits and cotton and negroes! and—other good things.

So I had a private sale at home, and sold my umbrella and overshoes, my overcoat and buckskin gloves, buffalo robe and fur cap, fur gauntlets and woolen undershirts, high top boots and heavy socks.

In short, I just dressed up in what I called a regular "Down South suit," low quarter shoes, thin, white socks, loose turn down collar and white cravat, a light straw hat, well perforated, and all things else to suit.

Well, I must go by the Centennial. I've started out to educate myself, and an education would be incomplete without taking in at least one Centennial, and as I might not get to the next one I must go now or never. Besides, I wanted to see my kinfolks. Some of them had been living over there about the Garden of Eden ever since our Father Adam first went to housekeeping. Now, as they had come so far, it would be discourteous not to meet them in the "City of Brotherly Love."

Don't you forget it, it suited very well for me to leave home on Sunday evening, and go by the little village of L——, that an early start might be made from that station next morning.

Now of course Pauline would not have gone anywhere without her father's permission; but it was rumored that he had a notion to send her off that evening, for fear she might want to go along to the Centennial.

It is Sunday afternoon. The sun hangs low in the west. The willow branches sway to and fro in the zephyrs that steal down from the densely shaded gorges where the crystal spray and foam dashes from cliff to cliff, forming a thousand rainbows from the sunlight that filters through the thick green foliage of forest oaks.

The small spring wagon stands at the stile with driver, trunk and valise aboard. Father and mother, sisters and brothers, stand around to give the last shake of the hand and imprint the final kiss upon the cheek of him whose moustache will be too much in the way for that when he returns.

The old dog gets up from his shady place and looks on with a sad countenance. The calf in the yard ceases to chew its cud, as much as to say: "I'm about to lose a mate." The ducks made out of the branch, and *quack*, *quah*, their final farewell. In fact everything movable and immovable seemed to sa -well, Brudder Jones."

The hills and dales, orchards and vineyards, soon shut from view the sweet home, with its hallowed influences which clustered so thickly about the old cottage. He is gone! Yes, gone to look no more upon these sacred scenes in five long years.

Oh! how sad are these partings. But perhaps you would ask what that had to do with my education. Well, it had a great deal to do with it. It's what Dr. Haygood calls "cutting loose from your mother's apron string." I have seen some young fellows in college who had not fully done that, and they made fools of themselves.

But when once away, I left off grieving and tried to make every sweet girl my sister, and every good woman my mother (in law) and thus learned to love the home of my adoption.

The shadows are lengthening, the village of L—— rises to view, the lights are beginning to glow as twilight sinks into darkness. Two young hearts meet on the piazza in the pale starlight once more to say farewell.

Now, just along here, many a fellow has given up the best purposes of his life and yielded to the sentimentality which evidently exists in great abundance on such occasions as these. Not so in this case.

"I leave you to-morrow morning, Pauline, on the early train, and it may be years before we meet again. The toil and anxiety which await me already burden my heart when I think upon what lies before me. But duty—that's the biggest word to me, now, in the English language—and duty says I must leave you. The injunction is, 'Seek ye first the kingdom of God and His righteousness, and all these things shall be added unto you'"—(such as wife and children, mother-in-law and old maid sisters, doctors' bills, shoemakers' bills, merchants' bills, leaky houses, lands, smoky stovepipes, sleepless nights when the baby has the thrush, or is teething, all this, with tribulation—when I revolved all this in my mind I felt "kinder" glad that these things were postponed rather indefinitely.)

"But, Jack, I'll be true, and the days and years will soon glide by, and you will be back again, never to be separated from me as long as life shall last."

There stood "two souls with but a single thought, two hearts that beat as one."

The day dawns, the train rolls into the little station, the whistle blows, the bell rings, and in an hour I am thirty miles nearer Philadelphia than ever before. Once upon the road, I throw myself back into the seat with a kind of an air of "I'm traveling."

Education consists, you know, of *varied informa- tion*, and to take a trip once in a while is a good thing. But this was my first trip.

Presently a young fellow spied me and he said to himself, "that's my chance." Picking up a basket he struck for me. Well, that basket! I had never seen the like before, and when he had got through with me I had bought a vegetable ivory needle case, a plush pincushion, a whistle, a tin horn, a rattle, a prize package of paper, a prize package of candy, a little gum thing you put over the mouth of a bottle filled with milk, a pocket saw-mill, a cross-eyed darning needle and a left-handed gimlet! Yes, sir, I did! Of course you say, "What made you do it?" Yes, I say "What made me do it, too?" I was getting my education. I don't do that way now. What made *you* do that way the first time you went from home? You did not know any better. That's the kind of a man I was.

But let me tell you; I traded those things off.

"What for?"

For a monkey.

"What did you do with the monkey?"

Ah! thereby hangs a (monkey's) tale.

Late in the afternoon, about 4 o'clock, we rolled into the prettiest city I had ever seen; when the engine settled down in Camden street station, I stepped out upon the beautiful streets of Baltimore.

As so many people have been to Baltimore and know so much more about the place than I do, I forbear describing the place. It is, indeed, a model city, and the little while I was there was a treat.

Next morning I started for Philadelphia. Leaving the city we soon came to the bridge that spans the beautiful Susquehanna. Ah! that grand old river, as it flows so gently, with scarcely a ripple, into the Chesapeake Bay, its banks lined with habitations, form a scene which inspires the youth with grand and elevated thoughts.

A few short hours' ride through elegant farms, dotted here and there with neat dwellings, large and well filled barns, beautiful plank fences all whitewashed, and clover stacks literally checking the green meadows, with cattle, sheep and horses grazing leisurely in clover knee high, and we were soon in sight of the city of William Penn.

I put up at the "Atlas Hotel," kept on the European plan—that is, you call for what you want and pay for what you don't get.

I did not want much of anything except a bed, and I didn't get much of that—just three slats and two sheets.

My good mother had filled one side of my valise with chicken and ham, pickles and cake, jelly and dried beef, hard-boiled eggs and apple pie, butter, biscuits, etc.

So, I did not want anything I saw at the Centennial (for I had plenty of toys) except one thing, a pretty little piano—I wanted it bad, I wanted it—to stop that awful bellowing and squealing.

This must have been the piano that Rubinstein played when the old countryman went to the city for the first time. I know it was the one they played the first time I went.

I did not exactly see the " stream of silver running over pebbles of gold, and the little white-winged angel leading the music away off down through the meadow, out of hearing, while the leaves of the bushes danced and bowed as it passed away," but I tell you what I did see—I saw two or three men and women holding the keys trying to lock the thing up and shut its mouth, and they could not do it. It just bellowed on. It was one of those grand, old steam " pianners" of the six driver-wheel kind, and it just moved right along, never stopping at any small stations for wood, water, coal, mail, or female. It was a *through fast mail.*

Well, I saw everything at the Centennial, the "world in a cocoanut shell." I have not seen but one thing since that I didn't see at the Centennial. That was my twenty-fifth birth-day—they didn't have that there.

It was strange to me that one could become so lonesome in so vast a crowd as that. But, among all the motley crowd of presidents, governors, statesmen, colonels, generals, 'squires, magistrates, kings and queens, earls and princesses, cardinals and archbishops, the "wise men of the east," the rich men of the west, the fool from all quarters of the globe, and Tom Walker, with not one man, woman, child, monkey or baboon into whose face I had the pleasure of looking, did I have the slightest acquaintanceship.

I was reminded of the beautiful words of Byron in Childe Harold, when he said :

"To sit on rocks, to muse o'er flood and fell,
To slowly trace the forest's shady scene,
Where things that own not man's dominion dwell,
And mortal foot hath ne'er or rarely been ;

How I Got My Education.

>To climb the trackless mountain all unseen
>With the wild flock that never needs a fold;
>Along o'er steeps and foaming falls to lean;
>This is not solitude, 'tis but to hold
>Converse with nature's charms and view her stores unroll'd."
>
>"But 'midst the crowd, the hum, the shock of men,
>To hear, to see, to feel and to possess,
>And roam along, the world's tired denizen,
>With none who bless us, none whom we can bless,
>Minions of splendor shrinking from distress!
>None that with kindred consciousness endued,
>If we were not, would seem to smile the less,
>Of all that flatter'd, follow'd, sought or sued,
>This is to be alone; this, this is solitude!"

I would not have been half so lonely with Pauline, under the June apple tree, as I was there in that park, among all those people and big houses.

I learned another thing at the Centennial, and that was that a "Guide Book" to an affair like that was just about as useful to a visitor as a foreign guide who speaks but one language would be to an American tourist in Europe.

Of course, I wanted to see everything and know where it came from—the author, the inventor, the designer and translator, who captured it, and how it was tamed, who wore it, and how long it was worn without washing, its size, weight, age, and capacity, cost of its importation and price of its history.

So I bought a Guide Book (yes, a *guide* book) to the Art Gallery, Machinery Hall, the Main Building, the U. S. Building, Horticultural Hall. the Glass Works, the Woman's Pavilion, the Men's "Distillion," the Turkish Bath House; one to the Cafe Mazerin, the Cafe Halle des Femmes, the Bonnee foi, the Rue Vivienne, the Cafe de *Rat Mort* (the cafe of the dead rat). I bought one to the Bois de Boulogne, another to Vaudeville, the Gymnas, the Palais Royal, the Ambigue, etc., and, finally, one to know how to get away from these places; and more finally, one to know how to get out of the grounds. "Every road leads to Rome," but the trouble was to find one that led from Rome. Well, I just *roamed* about.

But that wasn't all. I had to hire a guide to teach me how to use this library. I wanted an index to the indices. Moreover, while some invalids had to hire a three-wheeled chair to convey them from one place to another, it was more necessary that I should hire some one to carry my guide books.

Thank goodness, one may live and learn; and by the time I was ready to go to the Yorktown Centennial, five years later, I had learned not to buy guide books. I was guided then by the dust! I knew that where there was so much dust there must be something going on, so I followed the dust. Don't forget that, and never buy a guide-book if it's dusty.

Something else struck my fancy there, though, and I invested my spare change this time in Yorktown-

Centennial-Medals. They had 'em from ten cents up.

Leaving the Philadelphia Centennial, I found myself back in the city of Baltimore preparatory to starting for my new home in the South.

I had written to the general ticket agent of that city for prices of different routes, and had been informed by his excellency that the cheapest and best route was from Baltimore via Richmond, to Atlanta, Ga.

Stepping into the ticket office I called for one first-class ticket via Richmond to Atlanta.

"The recent rains, sir, have so demolished the route that a passage that way would be impracticable," said one of the sub-agents.

"Well, sir," said I, "you have written me that this was the route for me, and have specified the price, and I have governed myself accordingly; it would be impossible for me to retrace my steps via Staunton, Lynchburg and Dalton with the change I now carry in my vest pocket!"

"I guess you are mistaken, sir, about the information we gave you."

"I suppose not, sir; you had better look up your files and copied letters."

I just stood there, like Joe Brown's son, and asserted my rights with confidence. They began to investigate. The general agent came in, and the senior clerk, and after a while they rendered the verdict of—

"You're correct, sir."

"Yes, sir, thank you. What are you going to do about it?" and I stood right there.

"W-e-l-l," said the general agent, "I guess I—I'll have to fix you up a ticket;" and what do you think! That man fixed me up a coupon ticket that sent me eight hundred miles West, six hundred miles South, and two hundred miles East! all for less than twenty dollars. I was really glad it had rained so hard down about Richmond, so I could take a long route, all for the same money.

They called it an "emigrant ticket." I called it a kind of half-fare-free-ride-ticket. I hardly knew which way I was going; felt very much like asking them to tag me like a bag of wool, so if I got lost I could be returned to them, that they might start me out again.

That night about ten o'clock the emigrant took his seat, and all night long the old train rolled and rattled over hill and dale, spanning gorges and rivers, running under cliffs and through mountains, until daylight found us away out in the mountains of West Virginia. I was really going West when I meant to go South.

It was a wonder to me to see the coal and iron regions. The hills were dug and tunneled; the valleys were trestled and filled in; the houses were black, the trees were black, and the smoke and fog that hung like a curtain of night over these cities were almost impenetrable.

For miles and miles the railroad ran up and down the mountain, at times away up among the rocks and cliffs, with the Cheat River a mile below; then it would dart down and skim along the water's edge, giving one continual panoramic view of picturesque mountain scenes, filling the soul with music and poetry, which can only give expression in great sighs of "It's grand! Oh, it's wonderful!" That's all you can do.

But after awhile the green meadows, golden grain-fields, with bonnie lasses driving the reapers; fine orchards, rich, dark green cornfields, cosey country farm houses, and large white barns peculiar to the State of Ohio, literally crowded upon the view.

A short stop for dinner at Chillicothe, and Westward we rolled.

Late in the afternoon, just about sunset, the noise of factories, foundries, steam mills, the roll and rattle of carriages, omnibuses and drays, the smoke and steam from a thousand manufactories, the towering steeples and granite walls of elegant buildings—all told of our arrival in the "boss city of the West," Cincinnati.

Thirty minutes for supper and I knew nothing of the busy West. I lay down to sleep in Cincinnati and took breakfast in Nashville! I was emigrating rapidly.

It was not long after leaving Nashville till I knew I was getting down in the land of the "Sunny South."

The winding cotton rows, sweet potato ridges, peanuts and negroes, together with the absence of haystacks, meadows, spring houses, large barns, fat cattle and apple orchards, showed that I had changed base. This is no *base* contrast which I have drawn between the two sections, either.

Indeed, that day's ride was one of weariness to me. That part of the country from Nashville to Chattanooga, with the rain pouring down in torrents, till the cotton and sweet potatoes stood six inches in water, and the emigrants' car leaking, soiling his down South suit, presented a scene not much adapted to the feelings of a young tourist.

I sighed for my native "Blue Ridge Home" and the little town of L—.

But after awhile the sun broke forth, the mocking bird sang sweetly in the crab-apple tree, the zephyrs from the Gulf cleared the mist and fog from the sweet-winding Tennessee, which lay like a silver girdle around the base of Lookout Mountain and the city of Chattanooga.

I was really fascinated with the contrast, and when we struck the old State road with its solid ballast and steel rails, we shot like a swift-winged bird down past Dalton, Ringgold, Kingston (that's one time I did not stay long at Kingston), and when the whistle *rang* and the bell *blowed*, I stepped off the train in the little city of Cartersville, on Georgia soil for my first time.

Next day, when I sat down to sum up what I had learned on my first big trip, I found I had more experience than money.

CHAPTER III.

STUDENT, TEACHER, FARMER, AND AGENT.

I SHALL never forget the warm reception I received from my half-sister and brother-in-law, who had preceded me to Georgia three years. The door of their humble home was ever open to me, and it was through their instrumentality that I came to Georgia to work my way through college. Their house was my home for the next ten months.

Education being my purpose, I lost no time in making the necessary arrangements for entering school. I agreed to work night, morning and Saturdays in the garden and photograph gallery for my board.

I called on the Professor and asked him to credit me for my tuition, which he kindly agreed to do, and thank kind Providence for the many other kind-·

nesses I received at the hands of this true Christian gentleman.

I had six dollars in money. That being spent for books, I entered school with the determination to succeed. Longfellow says, "A boy's will is the wind's will," but with a strong tide of poverty beating against my every effort, together with a dull perception, growing out of the lack of early training, I battled and struggled until it was at last apparent that I had made some little progress in the road to learning. Slow and hard of necessity, though, is the march from chaos and darkness to order and light. Many were the weary hours I spent over the simplest lessons, while to others, with early advantages, they would have been quite easy.

But I labored under another great disadvantage—this was in a social relation. In Virginia, if a man is a gentleman, no matter what his calling, he is as much respected without title, as with title. The farmer, the blacksmith, the wheelwright, the miller, are all as highly respected as the lawyer, doctor, or merchant. Not so in Cartersville. Unless you are the son of a doctor, colonel, judge, lieutenant, major, 'squire, or something like that, or have some money, you had better emigrate "fudder."

So it seemed more congenial for me to associate mostly with my books, the result of which rendered me able, at the end of ten months, to find a place in the public schools as teacher. I thanked God and took courage.

Summer and autumn glided by without anything very unusual taking place, except the hat which I thought so perfect for the climate of Georgia proved a failure. The holes let the mosquitoes through, and I had to stuff cotton in the crevices to keep them out.

But, alas! winter came—a Georgia winter! It may be a little late, and just give you a small shower every few hours for about two months in the early part of that season; but do not be deceived—mud and rain are not all you will have. No, sir. The first winter I spent in Georgia the snow was six inches deep. It don't matter if the roses do bloom till December, you had better do like I did—get an overcoat, a pair of over-shoes, two umbrellas, (four to loan out—you will need yours all the time,) thick woolen clothes, woolen socks, hightop boots for snow and mud, a fur cap with ear flaps to it, and all such things as I sold in Virginia when I started to Georgia. It has actually been so cold on the coast of Georgia and Florida, that the fish have frozen to death and floated to the shore. But I never wrote anything like that to Virginia, I knew they would not believe it. But they know it is true in Georgia, but they don't like to acknowledge it. They are afraid it will injure the country.

But you say what has all this to do with how I got my education? Why, a great deal. I was studying geography—*climate!* There is more geography in a Georgia winter as regards *weather*, than in all the text books I ever saw. I actually wore my heavy clothes nearly out, pulling them off and putting them on, the changes were so frequent.

It's just a moral necessity to know geography (as to climate) in Georgia. One day the flowers will peep out, and the next day all is hushed and stilled into silence in the embrace of ice, snow and sleet.

Nearly a year had passed, vacation had come, and I must make some money to pay my debts. But alas! my clothes were threadbare, my hat seedy, my shoes worn, no credit established, no money in bank, no friends to assist, and to go out among strangers attempting to make up a school in that kind of an outfit, would have been to have failed and be classed as a tramp. Wear good clothes (not as a fop)—they are the best investment a young man can make, especially if he is among strangers. Dress neatly, hold a high head and go forward.

It is better to borrow enough to buy a good suit of clothes and make the money afterwards, than to attempt, half-dressed, to earn the money first.

"With all thy getting" get good clothes. So a dear, old brother (God bless him,) opened his kind heart and loaned me twenty-five dollars with which I dressed myself in a new suit from head to foot.

So off to the country I started to try my powers in teaching the young idea *how to shoot*. I walked most of the way and rode the other, till I found myself at last fifteen miles in the country.

It was one of those beautiful Georgia August days —not even a fly was stirring, it was so hot. Ah, me! these are the times that try boys' grit! Many of them give it up right along here! But two days' hard riding, and walking together, over hills and rocks, through persimmon bushes and black-jacks, and I had a school of thirty-five or forty pupils. One man subscribed five—and never sent them a day. He did it to encourage me in the outset. I thank him for it to this day.

Three months of hard work in the school-room, and I rode into town as independent as a section-master on a hand-car. I called round and paid the professor my tuition; called and paid the old brother the twenty-five dollars borrowed; gave my sister twenty-five dollars for good pay, and, in fact, I had a few dimes left in my pocket besides.

I went to school about five weeks, and vacation was over. My school opened again, and on I taught, and went to school alternately, until three sessions had passed.

It is one thing to teach and quite another to collect. You can collect children much easier than you can money. I recollect all I got from one man was an old musket and a "yaller dorg." I shot the dog and gave the gun away.

Two years had gone glimmering since I left the little village of L——. Not a line had I received from Pauline. We had promised not to write to each other—love, you know, dies out quicker if you don't write—and we were true to our promise.

But one October evening, as I strolled home from the school-house, tired and worn out from the labors of the day, faint of heart and weary of life (for my confinement as student and teacher had reduced me to a mere skeleton), I was handed a letter, light of weight but heavy in meaning, for on it I plainly read the post-mark of the little town of L——. I glanced at the address, and with trembling hands and heaving breast, I recognized the handwriting of Pauline!

The Chaldean king could not have been more puzzled to know the meaning of the strange writing on the wall than I was to know the purport of this little note.

"What could it mean? Is she tired of waiting and is writing for my return? They do get tired. Is it an invitation to her and Clarence's wedding? Oh! if that were so, let my epitaph be

"My love was false but I was firm
From my very day of birth;
Upon my body lie
Lightly, gentle earth."

"Was her father dead, and did they want me to return to take charge of the business for them? If that be true, I may go, though I may be required to walk.

"Must I tear it open and devour its contents, like some nervous woman? or shall I wait till after tea, and steal off in the twilight among the bushes, where nothing but the toad and katydid can see and be seen?" and I placed it in my side pocket and walked three times around the big chestnut tree which stood in the yard, and said, "Twice one is two (when you are single); twice one is one (when you are married)."

Then I stopped, took the thing out of my pocket, and was just about to tear it half in two, when the supper bell rang; and of course I put it back in my pocket, and walked in to supper, just like any other sensible man would do.

By the time I had eaten my supper I had forgotten I had the *thing*, and, lighting a choice cigar, I took a stroll with the young folks to get chinquepins.

About nine o'clock I happened to think of the strange visitor, and going to my room I shut the door and locked it, pulled down the blinds, took off my coat, rolled up my sleeves, roached back my hair, brushed the perspiration from my brows, and—sat down.

There wasn't much in it—a very small affair—but it counted:

"Hoping it may not cause you a moment's real sorrow, I feel it my duty to inform you that the promises I made you Sep'ember the 12th, 1875, can never be fulfilled. With many wishes for your future and eternal welfare, I remain,

Your true friend,
Pauline Prestine."

It was only two sentences, but of course that ended it. This would have been a fine time to have said, "Education aint much account, anyway; I'll quit." Many a boy has gotten off at this station and taken to the woods.

I said, "I'm sick anyway, and this stroke will end my existence. The green grass will soon grow over my grave, and my purposes and hopes will all have ended ere the white snows of another Georgia winter cover the roses.

I had it bad, don't you forget it. But—

> There's never a day so sunny
>   But a little cloud appears;
> There's never a life so happy
>   But it has its time of tears;
> Yet the sun shines out the brighter
>   When the stormy tempest clears.

> There's never a dream that's happy
> But the waking makes us sad;
> There's never a dream of sorrow
> But the waking makes us glad;
> We shall look some day with wonder
> At the troubles we have had.

By morning I felt that I would rather live than die. So I got a bottle of Simmon's Liver Regulator, two bottles of Cod Liver Oil, one pint of Honey Nectar, three bottles of Dr. Jayne's Ague Mixture, two ounces of Olive Tar, a little of Green's August Flower, one bottle of *Blue's October Blossom* and about a dozen spring chickens. Then I began to dose myself a little.

But all to no purpose. I grew thinner every day. I spent all the spare change I had on doctors' bills and patent medicines, and by the time school closed I had nothing in this world left me but a skeleton.

Then I thought of my father's house, of the many plows and harrows, hoes and rakes, mauls and wedges, cradles and scythes, which had given me such a good appetite, and so many pleasant nights of refreshing sleep, and I said, "I will cease feeding these little *lambs* on the dry husks of my dull brain, and will arise and go to the farm and say, "I am not worthy to be called a farmer, but just make me a digger of briars and a piler of stones, and patent medicines and doctors' bills will no longer drag me to poverty and ruin."

"Where there's a will there's a way," and if a boy is not too proud there are always avenues opening where he may enter and succeed.

It takes good grit, though, I can tell you. I shall never forget my old friend Union and the six months I kept "Bachelor's Hall," and worked on his farm.

Those were days of a peculiar kind of *education*; an education that may be needed in the future, when my "Pauline"—no! my "Susie"—no! my "Callie"— No! Well, when my—m-y wife is sick and the cook's away. (I was about to give myself away, then.)

Three months later and I was a picture of almost perfect health.

I had helped pick a crop of cotton, sowed a crop of wheat, hauled rails, made fences, fed the gin, fired the engine, milked the cow and cooked our "grub." Yes, sir, I could fry corn bread and bake ham, skin a chicken and stew eggs, *poach* coffee and toast biscuit, burn my fingers and scald my foot, just as good as any other little woman.

I used to get dinner on Sunday, then dress up in my long-tailed coat, walk leisurely across the fields, trimming the dough from under my finger nails, walk in on the piazza and take a seat by a white dress, and look just as innocent as though I did not know how she burnt her finger, scalded her foot and fell out of the kitchen door against the slop-tub, and let the beans boil dry, and the cat get her head in the cream pitcher, and the dog in the cupboard ; but I knew all the time, I'd been there. Education, you see, in the culinary department.

Well, I received only fifty cents a day in money, but five hundred dollars per month in health and experience. But when I had enough health and experience, I wanted more money.

Farming is good, teaching is better, but canvassing beats them all for making money and getting varied information. It isn't everyone, though, that can stand the first six months of a canvasser's or drummer's life. The experience is *too* varied. But if they can stand it that long, there is some chance for them to succeed.

Many a youth has wanted an education as badly as I did, but rather than undergo the trials and persecutions of such a life they retired in disgust and got married. (Then they got canvassed and curtain lectured, too.)

Success is not so much to the swift as to those who stick at the thing under persecution. The thing is to go in bravely—and stay there. So—

> Never let your chances,
> Like the sunbeams, pass you by;
> For you'll never miss the water
> Till the spring runs dry.

A New York man got hold of me, and like most Northern men, he knew his business, and was determined I should know it, too.

Whatever is worth doing is worth doing well, and to thoroughly know what you propose to do is more than half the battle. So I spent two months over a descriptive sheet, telling me how to show a book, and when that man was through with me I was really ready for business.

But I had to sacrifice a little false pride, right along here. Some of the dead-heads about the town said: "Ah! You're going to be a book agent, are you! You'll be classed with the tramps."

Then my time to speak came, and I said, " Yes, you're a tramp now; you tramp from your father's house down town, tramp back at noon ; tramp to the river and fish all day, and never bring back a minnow, tramp home and eat like a tramp ; don't earn a dollar in twelve months, and yet Solomon, in all his glory, didn't know as much as you do—in your own opinion. I'd rather be a successful tramp, and make something out of it, than be a failure at that. If I'm to be a tramp I'll be a first-class one and make a success of it." That's what I said. (They didn't put up the next speaker.)

I thought I saw, in the business just about to be entered, greener fields and richer pastures than I had been accustomed to graze in. So I waived prejudice, false pride, thoughts of failure, and all that, until there was nothing left me but success.

The dream of the little village of L—— troubled me no longer. When once Pauline had turned the current of her love into another channel, of course I ceased to grieve about spilt milk and sour grapes.

The gods had smiled on me again. Another fair maiden, a sweet-spirited, blue-eyed Georgian, Rosa Hawthorne, had promised to wait till I finished my college course. Such a lovely creation had never crossed my path before.

It seemed, indeed, strange that I should so unexpectedly meet this pure, unsophisticated country woman.

It was just inside or outside of North Georgia at a camp-meeting, or some other meeting, that I met this fair damsel.

I remember trying to tell her how she impressed me, and she was so still you could have heard a gum-drop.

"Miss Rosa, you are the cosiest little woman I ever saw."

"Mr. S——, I hardly understand the expression 'cosey,' I wonder if it's a compliment?"

"I am sure, Miss Rosa, you would think it complimentary could you see the meaning with which I endow the word. Imagine a beautiful little frescoed room with Brussels carpet, lace curtains, red shades; hanging pictures covering the walls; flowers blooming inside the window; a canary bird in a yellow cage hanging in the corner singing its sweet song; a centre table filled with periodicals and magazines; a large arm-chair softly cushioned; the glowing coals in the grate, ('Does this *grate* upon your ear? No, go on!') warming the room, while without the dark, blue clouds of a cold winter day hurl and dash the snow-flakes over the hard, frozen ground. View the little room in contrast with the dreariness of the outside world, and you have the definition of the little word *cosey*."

She caught on to that, and it wasn't long before I was living on hope again.

A good promise is a great thing. You don't know whether it will be kept or not; but you can live in hope. I had lived on just such a one several years before, and I could have that mirage to lead me on, if it never were overtaken.

The gate of active business life swung wide and invited me in. I entered. The fields were white unto the harvest to every one who would thrust in his sickle. Thank God for the generous spirit of the Southern business man who stoops down to help a poor, struggling youth in his endeavors for mental attainment. A thousand different avenues opened where one might enter and reap a rich harvest if he feared not the golden rays of the glorious sun.

I have traversed Georgia from mountain to sea coast, and in every valley and on every hill-top the wealth of a nation sleeps, waiting to be roused and put into action. Along her streams and in her valleys are seen the broad acres of productive soil, and is heard the music of a thousand factories.

Why should the young man not succeed? Why should he grow up in ignorance if he want an education, though he be poor? True, some men will try to frown you down and ridicule your early efforts to succeed. What if they do? None but the truly successful in any profession escape such rebuffs; then make yourself one of the successful and escape that which is unappreciated in your business.

I have stood on the banks of the Chattahoochee at Columbus, as it fairly dances to the music of the "Eagle and Phenix" mills, and there amid fierce competition, my efforts were crowned with success. I pressed my way through the busy streets of the "Gate City" with an eye blind to fashion and ear deaf to ridicule, my motto *labor omnia vincit*, and there honest toil reaped her reward.

Twelve months with its variegated experience as a book agent had passed; October had ushered in the beautiful fall, physical labor had said, "it is enough for the present, come up higher." Three thousand dollars worth of books having been talked into the people, I called my labors a success.

Then Emory College, God bless the old institution, opened wide her benign arms and welcomed her adopted son to her generous bosom. For the first time in my life I was what I had so often longed to be —a college student. While a college course will not make a smart man out of a fool, it is not all a mirage. The fountains and lakes, green oases and limpid streams which appeared in the distance to entice and lead on, were not all illusions. Much was real and all was valuable.

CHAPTER IV.

AT COLLEGE AND ON THE ROAD.

It is Wednesday morning, 10 a. m. October 5th, 18—. The whistle blows for Covington, the bell rings and a dozen students get off at the depot, and all pile in our hack for the little village of Oxford.

Each student has a dozen questions to ask the good natured hackman. But he has been asked the same questions a thousand times, and knows the answer without having to think a moment.

" Mr. H——, how far is it to Oxford ?"

"Just a mile, sir," is the kind reply.

"Who keeps the hotel?"

"They have no hotel, but every house in town is a boarding-house."

"Is Emory College right in town?"

"Well, just as much in town as the town is in Emory College; it's all hid over yonder in the thick foliage together."

The questions multiply and diversify.

"Where will I find the President?"

"Who examines a student in Greek?"

"Who in Latin?"

"Who has the prettiest daughter in town?"

"When does college open?"

And a thousand other just as important questions, and all answered with equal politeness.

On rolls the well-filled hack over the beautiful road—at this season of the year—and presently we halt in front of the little dove-colored post-office.

Who has ever visited Oxford and not gone away with the kindest and most tender recollections of the delightful little village?

The beautiful clay road that passes through the main portion of the little town, and on by the cemetery, is lost from view a mile in the distance, among the dense shadows of the forest that lies northward of the outskirts of the town.

Southward, the gently undulating landscape, gradually drooping for a half mile, and then rising and falling into hill and dale, and broad meadows, is lost beyond the limits of the city of Covington, in the blue rim that skirts the horizon. The sun rises from behind a ridge of thick pine forest, and hangs for a moment over the sparkling brook that plays its sweet, murmuring song in the meadows below.

Westward, the sun hides itself behind the tall forest oaks that encircle the beautiful grain fields and orchards of one of the village farms. On main street stand several little stores, with here and there the residence of one of the professors.

Back a little, on other streets, are seen the lovely cottages of these happy, courteous, Christian people. The green sward, carpeting the whole plateau with its downy softness; the tall oaks, locusts, cedars, with here and there a magnolia filtering the golden sunlight through their delicate green foliage, darkening, softening and blending the lights and shadows into a "fairy land;" the white, brown and dove-colored and pea-green cottages standing here and there, laughing with joy and gladness as they peep out upon the smiling day, and above, over all, the blue sky and the gentle, sweet-scented breeze, stealing like a dream into this Eden, fills the soul with a joy that is akin to angels' happiness!

Just a little to one side, in the denser oak grove, are lifted the heads of the college buildings. Gravel walks lead to every part of the campus, and a plain shaft, with an iron railing, rises in honor of the first President of the college, Ignatius A. Few.

A dozen columns would be inadequate to tell of the advantages of Emory College as an institution of learning. With its magnanimous president, its corps of efficient professors, its splendid buildings, and the religious influence permeating every department, it is to the young man seeking knowledge what a cool, bubbling spring is to a weary traveler in a barren desert.

When I arrived in Oxford one of the very youthful boys asked how many sons I had brought to college? I looked a little ancient among some of the small fry.

I took up my abode at one of the mess halls, in fact the only one in existence at that time; not kept in such elegant style as now, but better than the one near "Lion's Den," in the days of Dumas.

Two of us roomed together, did our own sweeping and making up of beds—a kind of bachelor's hall affair. Of course I felt perfectly at home. I had graduated in that department on the farm.

A bell rings. It is the hour for supper. Twenty boys gather around a long but bare-looking table. A black-eyed, black-moustached, sharp-featured little fellow sits at the head of the table.

"Well, Mr. S——," said this wit, "this is your first trip to Oxford?"

"Yes, sir," sipping my coffee with a pewter spoon.

"First time you ever boarded at a hall?"

"Well, not exactly."

"Now, Mr. S——, just make yourself at home. Help yourself to what you see and call for what you don't see, but call loud, for it's in Atlanta."

We had ham and grits for supper, and grits and ham for breakfast. It continued that way until I wished I had been born a Jew, that I might not be allowed to eat ham at all.

Then the diet changed. We got fish. And we had fish until I almost decided I was a whale living on smaller fishes. The change was too seldom, that was the trouble.

One of our boys—the poet—had eaten so many grits that his poetical dreams were on that subject. Sitting on the steps of the piazza, one lovely evening, his soul all inflated with the pure and beautiful, he soliloquized thus:

"O thou beautiful, silvery, pale-faced moon, you look like—like—a—a plate of grits!!!"

I entered the Freshman and sub-Freshman classes. I was behind in Greek and Latin. There was one thing I avoided, throughout my whole college course, like a child would fire; I had learned that in my ten months' course in Cartersville—*not to study too hard*. They never had to tell me one time, "Hold up, boy, you're ruining your eyes; you'll injure your constitution."

There are many pleasant occasions in a college course of a social and religious character that break the dull monotony of the class-room. Prayer meetings, experience meetings, Sunday-school teachers' meetings, public debates, private debates, evening strolls with or without company, base ball, marbles and leap-frog. College life, indeed, began very pleasantly for me.

Along toward the close of Freshman year we struck the brush and thicket of Geometry, many things in connection with which I never understood.

For instance, the worthy professor in that department asked us many questions on the subject of angles.

"Mr. A., what kind of an angle is that L?"

"A right angle, sir."

"You are correct."

"Mr. B., what kind of an angle is that?"

"An acute angle, sir."

"Mr. S., what kind of angle is that?"

"A left angle, sir."

Everything just roared. I never did know why they laughed so.

Another thing which the professor said was always a mystery to me, knowing the nature of students as well as he did.

"Young gentlemen, you must get around these theorems."

I took him at his word. I went round all I could. Well, we had gone on our journey for some time, climbing perpendicular heights, through horizontal plains, making many right, left, acute and obtuse angles, until we had gotten round a great many theorems.

Finally we all came up to the theorem known to college students as the "Pons Asinorum" or Bridge of Asses. Many had gone that way before.

It was necessary to cross that bridge in order to reach the *plains* of Trigonometry, the broad fertile fields of Analytical Geometry, the mountain slopes of Calculus, and finally in Astronomy to swing off into space among the stars. But I had borne well in mind the injunction of our worthy professor, and had gotten round many difficulties, both seen and unseen, and now I must be true to the injunction.

The long-eared fellows marched right up to the bridge, and while they were attempting to cross, I switched off down the river, and many miles below I found a pony, which I mounted—it had been ridden before and was gentle—and rode leisurely down beside the murmuring stream to where it was fordable, and in I plunged and reached the further shore in safety. But alas, alas! I had lost my direction, and not having a compass to direct my feet toward the plain road where the rest of the flock were, I camped for many days and nights, all alone in that dark wilderness, without the slightest hope of ever seeing daylight again.

But finally I decided that to remain was to die, and to go forward was but to perish, so mounting the little pony, I started. Every once in a while, on some eminence in my route, I would call out for my crowd, and away to the right I would get a faint answer, but too indistinct to determine its meaning or learn my proper direction.

The thickets and hedges barred and impeded my progress, but on and on I wandered! Leaving the beautiful and undulating plains of Trigonometry far to the right, catching only at times a faint glimpse of the green sward and square plateaus in front of the elegant octagonal-shaped dwellings, my little narrow, hemmed up path becoming less and less passable at every turn.

On I pressed, calling out occasionally from some high place on my route as the waving grain fields of Analytical Geometry lay far to the right. But, like Moses, I could only see them. I could not get there!

A faint voice could occasionally be heard to say: "Come this way; it's beautiful here in these rich fields."

Then, perhaps, a fainter voice would say, "stay where you are, there's nothing good here."

But "on, Stanley, on." I could see the mountain slope of Calculus loom up before me in the distance, with its waving branches and its crystal fountains sending out their silvery mist and spray over the fertile plains below.

Finally, after days and weeks of wandering in the maze and wilderness, I came out into the plain road, where the boys had camped awhile at the foot of the mountain of Calculus.

I never rode a pony again.

I sat down and listened to the stories of the boys—of where they had been and what they had seen, and how sumptuously they had fared, until I almost wished I had crossed the bridge with the rest of the troop.

On up the mountain we climbed and finally scaled the top, and inflating a balloon with astronomical gas, soared off among the stars.

We never could have gotten back but the balloon bursted, and each man having sufficient gas of his own manufactured to inflate his empty head, everyone let themselves down gently to earth.

Commencement approached; a few days intervening

before the regular exercises began, and not wishing to lose any time, I took a small volume, known as "Our Brother in Black," and went down to Madison to see what I could do in introducing him down there, but I returned next day with most of the colored brethren with me on the seat.

When commencement was over and vacation had separated the students into a thousand different fields, and had given them as many different vocations, I took up my abode in the beautiful city of Augusta.

Had I been going somewhere for pleasure, I should have sought a cooler place, but strictly business was my motto. While men sat in the shade with two palm-leaf fans in hand, drinking iced-lemonade, soda water, and a little rye mixed in, trying to keep cool; and the women up-stairs with their *mother-hubbards* on, avoiding society that they might keep from suffocating, and the young men emigrating to the "sand hills" at night to escape mosquitoes and malaria, I waded through the streets of that burning, broiling city under the fierce rays of the July and August sun, with much inspiration and a great deal more perspiration, and made in the neighborhood of fifteen dollars per day.

One way to keep cool, is not to stay long enough in one place to get hot—keep moving. I moved—a man who has to educate himself and make the money during vacation must move; he has no time to get hot.

It took just five thousand words to show my work, and to get a man to take that in, it must be given to him in quick doses.

I called on a gentleman down town and asked his permission to show him the work.

"Well," said he, "you can show it to me, but I don't believe in your Bibles and religions no way— they aint no good. I don't belong to any church and never expect to—there's no creed under the sun I believe in."

But I knew better, so I commenced on him thus: "This is Hitchcock's Analysis of the Holy Bible, or the whole of the Old and New Testaments arranged according to subjects, in twenty-seven books, together with Cruden's Concordance to the Holy Scriptures revised and edited by John Eadie, D. D., expressly for the Analysis. The Analysis is by Roswell D. Hitchcock, D. D., LL. D., President of the Union Theological Seminary, New York. The subjects are divided into twenty-seven different books, such as Scripture, God, Jesus Christ, Idolatry and Superstition, Works of God, Mediums and Methods of Revelation, Duties to God, Angels, Good and (I'll be d— if I believe anything you are saying) Evil, the Family, Fallen Man, Man Redeemed, Hell, Heaven, The Judgment. Here are two hundred and fifty chapters, twenty-three hundred sections, six thousand subjects, an Interpreting Dictionary, a Pronouncing Dictionary, Scripture Measures, Weights and Coins, a Family Record, History of the Bible, (that's the only good thing in it—with an oath) and a Dictionary of all Religious Denominations, Sects, Parties and Associations in the World!"

All this was said in about a minute. When I showed him the "Dictionary of the Different Denominations" he said, with a double oath:

"Now, sir, please show me my sect of people and I'll buy a book."

"Very good," said I, and turning to it I read:

"*Yezides, from Yezid, founder of their Religion, called also Devil Worshippers—a singular people found in Turkish Armenia (more than 200,000), in Khoordistan (about 4,000), and in some other localities, who treat the Devil with scrupulous respect because they anticipate his restoration to heaven where they wish to have him for a friend.*"

When I got through, he said:

"That's my sect; I'll take a book."

All men have creeds and beliefs and doctrines; most of them believe in God. *There is no unbelief.*

"Whoever plants a seed beneath the sod
And waits to see it push away the clod,
 He trusts in God.

"Whoever says, when clouds are in the sky,
Be patient heart, light breaketh by and by,
 Trusts the Most High.

"Whoever sees, 'neath winter field of snow,
  The silent harvest of the future grow,
      God's power must know.

"Whoever lies upon his couch to sleep,
  Content to lock each sense in slumber deep,
      Knows God will keep.

"Whoever says, 'To-morrow,' 'The Unknown,'
  'The future,' trusts that power alone
      He dares disown.

"The heart that upward looks when eyelids close,
  And dares to live when life has only woes,
      God's comfort knows.

    "There is no unbelief,
  For day by day and night unconsciously,
  The heart lives by that faith the lips deny,
      God knoweth why!"

Never pay any attention to what a man says about his belief. Preach the word in season and out of season, something will strike him, and you'll win him over.

The summer is waning; the nights are more pleasant; the days are less boiling; business has been elegant, thirteen hundred dollars' worth of books have been sold to believers and non-believers.

I am nearer the ocean now than ever before, why should I not see it?

It is just a week after an awful storm has swept the Atlantic coast from Florida to Maine. The dead bodies of rice-farm servants are floating in mid-ocean.

Savannah is a mere brush-heap, interspersed with tin roofing blown from the dwellings. Tybee Island peeps out from beneath the debris and white sand of over rolling waves.

Everybody along the coast is drinking salt water, because of the mighty incoming of the tide. Towboats and schooners and fishing gulls and little sail boats stand on end, half-buried in the marsh, along the harbor. Men are hauling cord-wood and burning brush from the ruins of magnolias and cape jasmines. The storm is hushed into silence, and the elements look on the scene of destruction with an air of perfect innocence.

How bright and beautiful the early days of this September morning. I step upon a little tow-boat that expects to cross the bar and leave a ship to find its way to South America.

The sunbeams kiss the silvery waves of the Savannah as they waltz around the little steamer; the gentle zephyrs ift the white foam and dash it into a thousand glittering particles over the tottering little puller.

The floating clouds that promenade the horizon toward the East beckon us toward the music of the rolling deep. Chuck-a-chu, chuck-a-chu, chuck-a-chu, chuck-a-chu, goes the little propeller, and the great vessel with its mighty cargo follows. We cross the bar and the breeze strikes the sails of the old ship; she rides upon the waters like a thing of life.

"Halt, up, down, round, sidewise, around and around! Oh! splash! dash! asuh! bouah! My h-e-a-d hur-hur-t-s me clean down to my—Oh! heels, ooh! booh! Give my pocket-knife—augh!—to my little brother! boo! hoo—hem!—and my chewing gum to my youngest sister—augh! Oh! C-a n-t you s-q-u-e-e-z-e a l-e-m-o-n i-n some water and let me pass off easier ?"

"You're feeling badly, aint you ?" said the Captain.

"Do-o o-n't ask a dy-in-g man such a question as that, and tantalize his s-o-u-l—ough!—in that style. B-a-a-d is no name for it!!!"

Traveling is a good thing for a young man. Whatever is in him is pretty sure to come out—if he rides on a stormy sea.

CHAPTER V.

MY TRIP TO VIRGINIA.

Five long years of toil, weary waiting and anxiety, had glided by since I had said "Good-bye, Blue Ridge Mountain Home."

None but a fond mother and loving sisters can fully

appreciate the many heart-aches and heart-throbs experienced by a strange boy seeking his goal in a strange land. To them he owes much for sympathy, of which the outside world knows nothing.

The summer with all its heated labors is over; cool, balmy September draws its mantle of eloquence and poetry about me. The cars stand under the shed at the Union Depot; one long, loud whistle, seeming to sound half-way across the continent, stirs one anxious heart. The weary boy ascends the steps of the moving train, lays himself down to sleep in Georgia and wakes up in Virginia!

Home again! Heaven bends with all its blessings to welcome back the prodigal boy!

The old weeping willow droops its mournful head in humble silence at his coming. The cool, bubbling spring reflects the same bright, happy faces it did the Sunday evening he quaffed his last cooling draught from its crystal fountain. The old mountain branch sings the same sweet song it did the day he crossed it and said, "Sing songs to my mother in my absence." The blue-eyed Massanutten Mountain looks down through the thin gauze of a beautiful September day with its dreamy eyes and says, "I have stood here in all thy absence and watched over thy cottage home. I have stretched my shadowy wings to shield thy loved ones from the scorching rays of a mid-summer's sun, and from the stormy blasts of December's darkest days."

The pure mountain air that steals in among the cedars whispers the same holy prayer it did when first the youth bowed around the family altar to pay his devotions to the God of his fathers.

How inadequate are words and sentences to express the feelings of a returning wanderer, as he drinks in the sweets of a beloved and happy home!

The boy throws himself down on the green turf, under the willow by the spring, and all he can utter from the great deep of his soul is "*God is love!*"

The clearest view we can possibly get, though dim it may be, of the home in "Our Father's House," must be to enjoy the blessings of a sweet Christian earthly home. That is really and truly akin to heaven.

My little cottage home stood there in all its attractiveness, just as it did five years previous. No dark shadows had fallen across the doorway to mar the happiness of him who had been so long absent. How many bright flowers had been culled from the bouquets of other homes and family circles since I had left mine! But Providence had dealt so kindly with those I loved that not to be grateful would have been to have proved untrue to my better nature.

Now, where do you think I first stopped when I arrived in Virginia?

At the little village of L—. Getting off at the station, I took my valise in hand and marched up to the familiar mansion where I had spent three years of my early life so pleasantly, and before Pauline knew of my arrival I stood once more in her presence.

What her thoughts were then could be imagined only by the alternate blushes and smiles that played upon her comely face.

No one would have dreamed, from her bright face, that Clarence had pressed his suit in my absence, had been successful, and before the happy day had arrived had suddenly died. But that was even so. Clarence Morton had found a premature grave, and had left Pauline without a special lover.

Yet there were no traces of sorrow on her young, joyous face that September evening, as I stood before her, after the long absence of five years.

Perhaps there was some additional attraction about me. I wore a long-tail coat and heavy moustache; had been to college, studied Geography (Georgia winters) and Rhetoric; had learned beautiful sentences which breathed forth eloquent climaxes—

> "Oh dear, oh dear, what shall I do?
> I've lost my wife and seed-corn too!"

Had studied the languages (not much, though), was familiar with
> "Amo, amas, amat;"

and

"Ζώη μοῦ νὰς ἀγαπῶ."
could converse with my sweet-heart in German—

"O bleib' bei mir und geh' nicht fort, Om meinen herzen ist der schonste ort." I had been out of hearing of my mother's dinner-horn, had seen the white cotton fields of the South, and heard the sweet songs of the mocking bird, mosquito and sand-fly.

Now was a good time to bring my powers to bear upon the fair maiden again.

Many were our rambles over the clover fields and through the orchards, gathering the rich, golden fruit that was so fast ripening in the glowing sun of that lovely autumn.

Church services, pic-nics, camp meetings, Yorktown Centennials were taken in by us. Our constant association with each other brought back the dream of early love, and the vision of Rosa Hawthorne faded from my memory like the dew before the morning sun.

"Absence conquers love." I had been absent from Rosa a few days, in the presence of Pauline, and I was clear gone.

Many of Virginia's beauties I had never seen, and I must now avail myself of the opportunity to see some of her wonders.

The first place I visited was Weyer's Cave, one of Virginia's historical attractions, a few miles south of

Port Republic, in against one of the small spurs of the Blue Ridge system, and about seventeen miles north of Staunton, in Augusta county, is this wonderful cavern. Stopping at the residence of the owner of this cave, about a half mile from its entrance, we procured a guide, and, winding up to its mouth, we entered to behold what nature had done beneath the earth's surface.

A chill creeps over one upon entering, and he feels an intensity of awe as he looks beyond the dim, flickering light into the profound darkness that spreads its impenetrable gloom in the distance.

But a good guide, with the proper attendants to point out the road and reveal the beauties that stand like ghosts in their fairy-like abodes, is the delight of the visitor.

Passing down a long descent, we came to the Ghost Chamber, at each end of which two single, mute, stark-white sentinels stand as though they were guarding and receiving the countersign from passing spirits.

A few paces forward, and down a rude flight of some twenty steps, we reach the Cataract, seemingly a waterfall petrified in its leap over the precipice. The sudden stillness of this hushed Niagara makes one feel that he had been suddenly ushered into the presence of the green waters of the true cataract, and found it taking a quiet nap.

Leaving this grand representation we come suddenly into the presence of a political scene. There is the Senate Chamber, with the speaker's chair, the desks of the honorable members, and above all, at one side in the gallery, fenced round with a fanciful railing, over which seemingly peep and peer the heads of listening visitors.

Then comes the Cathedral, from the center of which hangs the fanciful resemblance of a beautiful chandelier, and above it rises the pulpit, an elevated desk covered with the most graceful folds of white drapery, and the ceiling literally covered with glittering crystals and sparkling stalactites, dropping in long points and broad, wavy sheets of milky whiteness; others of a muddy red, bordered with white or with the darker cornelian shades of the Piedmont brown.

On and on, from one beauty to another the visitor is led, while the guide tells his tale and reveals the similarity of three strangely formed objects to those we have seen by the light of the sun on the surface of the earth.

Washington's Hall, with its high ceiling of ninety feet, and its immense length of two hundred and fifty feet, with a large statue draped in courtly robes standing in the center of this spacious apartment, fills one with thoughts too grand for utterance.

We begin our expressions of wonder and surprise,

and leave them unfinished, just as nature seems to have done in her freaks in this intensely beautiful palace!

The thing that most especially struck my fancy was the "bridal veil," a most splendid sheet of white, glittering, translucent spar, which seemed thrown over a hat or the back of a large *tuck comb* and hung in long wavy folds, almost reaching the clay-red floor of this chamber.

I looked and looked, but alas! alas! in vain, the *bride* was not there, and I availed myself of the opportunity to say to a fair maiden who stood by me, that now would be a good time to enact another bridal scene, but she wouldn't be bridled.

Thus it is we are led from narrow passages to wider and more extended apartments, over precipices and tumbling pilasters, glittering stalactites and crystal fountains, till one is so lost in wonder and amazement that he wishes for daylight to reveal whether or not he has left this terrestrial globe.

Weyer's Cave is really one of the wonders of the new world, and is considered as such by all who view it in the light in which I saw it that glad day. A dozen pages could not fully describe the attractions of this wonderful place, so I pass on.

Among Virginia's wonders of recent date, are the Luray and New Market "endless caverns," the latter of which I was permitted to visit. Just a few differences I notice between this and Weyer's Cave.

In the New Market endless caverns, situated about three miles south-east of New Market, near the Massanutten Mountain, there is the additional beauty of newness. None of the exquisite formations have been effaced by the hand of the tourist, nor smoked up by the torch; all is clear, bright and sparkling; moreover it is acknowledged by visitors, that this cave possesses one beauty that none other has—the "Diamond Lake."

The mode of access to this attractive place is very difficult on account of an exceedingly narrow passage, the shelving rocks coming so near together as to necessitate crawling on the hands and knees to reach it, and finally to lie down and snail it for a few feet.

But ah! when it is once reached, you are amply repaid for all your trouble. The treat is worth crawling a mile to behold, it is such a wonder.

The little lake is about ten feet square and about a foot deep, with perhaps six inches of water clear as crystal; up through this water peep a million sparkling diamond stalagmites.

When the guide struck a match and lighting a magnesium ribbon held it over this fairy fountain, the sweet voice of a lovely female, sounding from the entrance through which I just had crawled, asked me if

I would not like to live there always. With her, I could have stood it awhile, but it would have been too damp around the edges to have remained long. To fully appreciate this beautiful scene one must make a comparison.

On some mountain during the night it snows; the snow is heavy and it rests on the limbs and bushes; before day-dawn the clouds pass off and it becomes cold and clear, a heavy frost settles on each separate limb and twig and particle of snow; the sun rises and sending its beams through these natural lenses, forms a million sparkling diamonds, making one vast, glittering, sparkling, spangled chandelier.

If you have seen this, you get a faint idea of what the Diamond Lake is in the New Market endless caverns. It beggars farther description.

Many were the pleasant visits I made on my trip to Virginia. But a month's deep, holy associations with loved ones, with its recreative powers of mind, body and soul, and I turn again toward my new home in the land of the sunny South.

Taking with me my sister, Pauline and several other ladies, I came by Yorktown, the birth-place of our nation, and trod the holy ground where once our fathers fought for liberty and conquered.

It was a grand place; grand, though, only in imagination, for it consisted simply of the old St. John's church, a few bar rooms, and—dust!!

We were there in a common cause and were all on an equality—all equally dusty, no distinction of color because of the dust.

But this, indeed, is the celebration of a notable time in the history of our republic. Standing on the heights looking over the river, white with the sails of almost every nation on the globe, each flag playing in one common breeze of liberty, the variegated curtain of a hundred years parted, and I gazed down the vista of the past, and beheld with amazement the mighty contrast.

Seventeen hundred and eighty-one, an infant nation just born!

Eighteen hundred and eighty-one, a giant in full glory!

The old ship of state has ridden well the current over the breakers, and as she sails into the broader and deeper seas, she has enlarged her rigging, spread her full sails, and so she will skim the wide waste of waters till she anchors on the placid surface of eternal peace, the pride of the world—America!

Coming back by Richmond, we found the Fair in progress, and the girls concluded to stay. So I had to say good-bye to Pauline once more.

But this was not half so sad as our former separation. I had a sweetheart if I stayed, and one if I did not stay. So I said, "Good-bye to you all—Miss Pauline," and shaking her hand tenderly, and looking at her very closely in the mouth I was gone again to live on hope—Oh, hope!

"Hope springs eternal in the human breast."

I wasn't married, but always hoped to be.

The next place I touched was the Atlanta Cotton Exposition.

They had guide-books there but I didn't buy any. They had vegetable-ivory needle cases, plush pin-cushions, rattles, whistles, incubators and the Little World; cross-eyed darning needles, left-handed gimlets and pocket saw mills, but I did not invest.

But I tell you what I did buy. A sharp Yankee found out, somehow, that I was a college student, and he said:

"This way, my friend."

I went. Patting me on the shoulder, he said:

"Aint your eyes somewhat affected by hard study? Don't they pain you, and get very tired at night after poring over your books till eleven and twelve o'clock at night?

(I tell you that sounded mighty refreshing.) I said:

"W-e-l-l, y-e-s, I—I believe they do."

"I thought so," said he, "you look like a hard student."

(Oh! that touched me all over.) Then he said,

"I've got the best eye-glass you ever saw; it will rest your eyes like a top."

(He had hold of some Emory boys before, and knew who he was talking to this time.) I said,

"My friend, do you think one pair with a nice little black cord will be sufficient for my o-v-e-r-w-o-r-k-e-d eyes?"

"Yes, if you wear them carefully and shade your left eye with your hat rim pulled down on one side, and carry your cane under your left arm, and hold your head a little to one side. This pair at two dollars and a quarter will suit you very nicely."

"All right," said I, "I'll take them."

I wore those glasses that day—those resters—and gave them away to the first old maid school teacher I met who wanted to look learned. A man must pay for his education, sure.

But I made a bigger bust than that at the Atlanta Exposition (I *bussed* the wrong girl).

Walking arm in arm with one of my college mates, taking in things generally, I suddenly passed a beautiful young lady, brown-eyed, dark, wavy tresses and fair to look upon, with unusually familiar-looking face.

I stopped suddenly and said to my friend,

"Joe, I know that woman, but where I have seen her I cannot tell."

I studied and thought till all of a sudden it came into my mind that it was my friend, Miss Irene Rosedale, who had accompanied me through the New Market Endless Caverns, and whose brown eyes had haunted me like a pleasant dream ever since. I turned from Joe Quillian to speak to the passing maid, but alas! she had gone from my presence like a June-bug from a 'tater vine. The rest of that day I put in looking for the brown-eyed maiden until hope had fled.

But late in the afternoon, in the Art Gallery, I suddenly came up with the fair miss, and in my joy I took off my hat, approached her as gracefully as a dancing master, extended my hand and bowed low. She clasped my hand tenderly in her white hand, and smiled as sweetly as an infant's laugh. Then I said in warm tones,

"How do you do?"

She smiled louder, and then I said again,

"This is my friend, Miss Irene, of Virginia, I believe?"

Then I saw a kind of half surprise and half sorrow and half joy, mingled with about one-sixteenth disgust, play "hide and seek" among the roses and dimples in her pretty cheeks. She said,

"You are mistaken, sir,"—(though she was really the *miss taken* for another).

Well, I bowed, stepped back and said,

"Excuse me, if you please."

How I Got My Education. 89

I was sorry I was mistaken, but very glad I had made the mistake. It did me good to shake hands with so pretty a girl and see her blush because she had done so without an introduction.

I have often wondered who and where and when and how she is, but never a line has she ever written me since I made her acquaintance in the Art Gallery at the Atlanta Exposition that beautiful October evening in '81. Friendships made on short acquaintance sometimes last but briefly.

On to Oxford I went and fell in line with my class and met the regular duties of a college life, with its sunshine and its show, its hopes and its fears, its joys and sorrows, filling up another college year with the study of text-books and writing letters to Pauline. Letters to and from the little village of L— came and went rapidly, and the carelessness upon my part, in the multiplicity of business, became a little too monotonous to the independent disposition of Rosa Hawthorne.

Rosa's soft blue eyes and gentle disposition did not divest her of womanly independence, and no one was more ready to resent and mildly rebuke an injury than she.

She brought me to taw about my carelessness and because I could not answer satisfactorily she said, "We will play 'quits.'" Well, we just quit, and that ended the matter. A handsome young doctor was paying his devotions to Rosa, and she was as independent of me as I was devoted to Pauline.

Love matters get wonderfully mixed up, anyway. They are as uncertain as the color of a next spring's style of dress goods.

CHAPTER VI.

ON THE ROAD.

This is a progressive age. In the world's busy thoroughfare, men and things are moving rapidly. The day of active business life is upon us, a day when the false theory of "luck" has given way to energy, mental and physical action.

The time for taking in school at sunrise and teaching till dark is gone with the things of old fogyism. The six-horse teams with the great red wagon body filled with bacon and flour, on the road to market a month, no longer claims the time and taxes the patience of the farmer. A week's transactions of former days are now performed in a few hours. Railroads, steamships, telegraphs, telephones, bicycles, tricycles and one wheel buggies have so connected the commercial, social, political and religious world that all are now neighbors.

How I Got My Education.

The farmer raises his products and sells them in some distant market without leaving his home. The South Georgia truck farmer grows early and late watermelons, and sends chills and fever to every city in the North without leave or license.

The retail merchant buys his goods from the wholesale merchants without either leaving their places of business.

The day of round-eyed axes, flails, sickles and spinning jennies have gone forever. This is a fast age, and men to succeed must be active and wide awake.

America builds churches, colleges, almshouses, and preaches the gospel in China and Mexico and Japan without one out of a million seeing the land of the heathen. The white bear of the North cordially shakes the alligator of the South by the tail, and they call each other neighbor.

As much of the labor as possible is performed by the men who stand at the head of their particular callings, and then when help is needed they seek the best material possible to transact their business. Young men, nowadays, to be useful must be educated men, not only theoretically but by practical observation, and a close study of what now moves the world.

Business—and when I say business I mean everything, even *selling a book*—is done on the wing, and those who are not good marksmen will stand but little chance for any game. The commercial world needs first-class business men, for most of the business is now done *on the road.*

There is or has been a false theory which prevails among many good people with regard to men who transact business on the road and are called "drummers" or "agents."

In the first place, they do not know what kind of people the general class are, whom they are continually abusing. True, some few men who travel justly merit the name of "wag," "sharper," "second-class man," "tramp," etc., and it is this few out of the 180,000 traveling men of the country, who have perhaps lowered this class in the eyes of the local traveler.

It is unfair to judge so many by the exceptional few. Because some preachers do wrong, does that degrade all ministers? Because some merchants fail with full pockets, and cheat their creditors, is merchandising no longer respectable?

Would that the intelligent world were charitable enough to consider who the great body of this traveling class are! The question will soon be asked no longer, when the bus starts to the train, "Are you going for a gentleman or a drummer?"

The men who travel now are men of intelligence who represent wealth and influence; men travel who are the heads of the largest banking, mining, railroad and commercial firms in the United States. Merchants and merchants' sons travel; bankers and bankers' sons travel; publishers and publishers' agents travel; ministers, lawyers and physicians travel, and transact their business from one end of the continent to the other.

Because one umbrella tramp comes along, takes your silk umbrella to put a new rib in it and never returns it, don't class all traveling men as such.

Young men of the first families have spared neither time, talent nor money in preparing themselves for the great business which is done on the road, and, as a rule, none but first-class men can fill these important positions. A second-class man soon loses his place and has to seek a commoner position in the business circles. One kind of business is just as honorable as another, and sometimes more so, just so it is honest, though it be nothing but selling a book.

If we could only learn the lesson that "whatever is worth doing at all is worth doing well," there would be less discredit reflected upon many callings, and less failure in working out the great problem of life.

If a man is so unfortunate as to have the lowest and meanest occupation life can afford, it is his duty to make the standard of that particular calling the very highest that his most skillfully exerted powers can make it. If his profession be that of a boot-black, then his greatest success lies in the power to persuade men that the very highest type of gentility demands that they patronize him. When he does this, and does the best job his skill can do, he makes that business a success.

If a boy's early life be that of a "newsboy," then he should learn what is in his paper and strive to impress upon every passer-by, whether he be lord or slave, that what he fails to read in this paper he may never see in another. When he learns to do this he has the secret of success in that occupation.

But if, on the other hand, a man has been more favorably situated, and had kind fortune to smile upon him, lift him up from the commoner walks of men and things, and exalt him to that high position so few attain; if she has bestowed upon him the marked distinction which the honor of being a book-agent brings to her favored few, why surely he has, above all men, a work of incalculable magnitude, and should fill with proficiency his worthy position, that his character in such a profession may reflect credit on all who come after him.

I have learned not to look down with scorn and derision upon a man in the commoner walks of life, no matter where I find him. Though he be but an humble lawyer or a politician, I know that, aside from the many heart-aches and heart-throbs that come in the disappointments of clients and offices, there are many green oases in the great desert of this life, where he may rest and eat his pone, which those in higher places, on account of the multiplicity of orders, and the countermanding of orders, and the " I-don't-want your-books," never experience. These men of commoner professions scarcely ever have to come so intimately in contact with the busy current of active life, they know not of what the world is made.

But if a man wants to know what he wished he had not known, let him wade out into the current of life, into the busy thoroughfare of men and things, and turn his face toward the source of the stream, and, in this condition of human events, meet men with small satchels and magazines, newspapers and chromos, and insurance policies and lightning rods, and analyses and patent churns, and patent bustles and patent corn medicine, and patent bustles and patent eye-wash, and men with big trunks and men with little trunks, and "Mark Twain on the Mississippi," and the Life of John Brown, and the New Revision, and then—if he don't smell sulphur about his garments, he is grit.

Filling a position on the road is an important calling, if it be but to sell a book. Most any one-horse clerk can stand behind the counter and measure off calicoes and weigh out hog and hominy to parties who want such things; but to sell a man, and especially a woman, a thing which they at first declare they do not want, is that part of business which discloses the secret of success.

In the first place they must go where business calls —through heat and cold, through sunshine and shower, sick or well, in the face of opposition and fierce competition. The motto to be written over the door of the man who goes on the road, and which greets his eye every morning is, "go! go! g-o-o-o!!!"

One poor fellow who started out with a line of samples, found that every place he went some one else had just been there with the same line of goods. He wrote to his house that if some one was not just ahead of him selling the same kind of goods, he could do well. The house wrote him to pull on, as there were eight thousand just behind him. I have actually made twenty dollars some rainy day while others were smoking cigars and waiting for the "clouds to roll by." Go! go! go! is the secret of success to the agent or traveling man.

The next best thing is to "possess thy soul in patience." There are many things going to and fro, up and down in the world, and if you are not a Job, you will lose your track. One often becomes worried, fatigued and tired of his way, sits down by the wayside to rest and wishes he had never entered the field. Some fool stands by the lists as the successful knight

How I Got My Education.

passes, and cries "hold! there are no laurels for you; there is nothing worth your efforts," when in reality he knows nothing about it, he has never been in the arena himself, has never made an effort worthy of success. But you will meet with this class all along your route.

Then comes your pleasant acquaintance with the railroad and livery stables.

Railroads are good things. They do much for us in the way of quick passage and fast freight. But it really seems that sometimes the railroad forgets that we are as much benefit to them as they are to us. Really, we could live without railroads, but they could not live without us. They seem to forget *that* when they are dealing with a traveling man.

Now, anybody is allowed one hundred and fifty pounds of baggage, whether he be a traveling man, tourist, or free negro. But men who transact business for railroads are scrupulously conscientious about baggage if it looks like it belongs to a traveling man. If he thinks it weighs one hundred and fifty-one pounds, he has it weighed and charges double first-class rates on that one pound, and asks the traveling man to help weigh it.

They check your baggage to a certain place, carry it on, keep it a week, then "cuss" you for not having followed it up. They carry your goods on to another town because your name looks like some other man's, and when you make them bring it back they get mad because your name was not something else.

They forget that traveling men buy their tickets at the office and pay for them as others do, and pay for excess of baggage as other people do. But they say, "Oh! he's a drummer, and hasn't time to argue with us; we will treat him as we please. He's a nuisance, anyway."

They forget that the traveling man does more for the railroads than any other class of people who travel. Thousands, yea, millions of tons of freight are going to and fro over these roads which have been sold by the drummer. They get the benefit of his labors and then "cuss" him for the little hand valise that sits by him on the seat.

Showmen come through the country, charter their cars, get reduced rates, pass through once, and drain the country from mountain to sea coast, yet the railroad authorities can't see the difference between the two classes.

Then you've got to walk the chalk, I tell you. If you ask any of them a question he will snap your head off.

Then, again, if a man gets too hot, which he often does in the summer time in a close car, and pulls his coat, shoes and socks, and washes his feet and hangs his socks up to dry on the seat in front by the side of a bride and groom, why they get hopping mad, pull the rope, ring the bell, blow the whistle, and actually *put him right out!* in a swamp, too, among the frogs, sandflies and mosquitoes, leaving him to find his way to the next station as best he can.

When a poor tramp, tired and weary, wants to steal a little ride in an old guano car, they run off the track and scare him nearly to death. If he gets on the truck under a car, in order to ride to the next station, they pull him out because he "might fall and stain the track with blood."

If a man is tired and sleepy, and lies down on the seat and puts his muddy feet up on the nice cushions, the conductor comes along and wakes him up, right in the midst of his most pleasant dreams. Oh! what cruel men!!!

Then they won't let a nice old lady smoke her sweet scented pipe (that hasn't been burnt out for three years) unless she goes into the smoking car, and she's too timid for that, and so the "poor old critter" has to go all day long without a smoke. Ah me! there's a judgment day coming for all such—old women.

Then come hotels, boarding houses and restaurants. It sometimes seems that people think that anything, at any time and any place, is good enough for a "drummer" and too good for a *book agent*.

How I Got My Education.

I am often reminded of Sut Lovingood's first sermon, when he said, "Stop not whar thar am a sign, but gird up your coat tail and marvel fudder, lest you lose your soul a cussin and have your paunch eat into a thousand pieces."

They light you to bed with a small piece of tallow candle, and wait till you retire to get the stump to make gravy for breakfast; and put bugs in the bed that you may rise early so they can have the sheet for a table-cloth.

As to prices, some of them haven't any—they just find out how much you have and take the whole pile.

A gentleman sat by me some time ago at a hotel table and fixing his eye on a plate in the center of the table, he said,

" Come here, come here!"

" What are you calling ?" said I.

" That dish of butter; it's strong enough to walk and soft enough to run."

He was a daisy—so was the butter.

A dish of chicken passed around the table and when it got to a drummer he said,

" Did you have much trouble holding that dish ?"

"No," said his friend, " why do you ask that?"

" Well, I see that it is all wing, and I thought likely it tried to fly away."

Many times when you inquire of a waiter when things look scarce, if he has any eggs, he will say,

"No, boss—jess out."
"Have you any syrup?"
"No, sah—jess out."
"Have you any milk?"
"No, sah—have some to-morrow."
"Have you any salt and pepper?"
"No, sah—dat's out too. Oh, yes sah; yes, sah, we has dat. Yes, sah—uh, yes, sah."

They just have their mouth fixed for "No sah, jess out," and that's all they know.

But there are many exceptions to this kind of treatment, which I would not pass unnoticed; many reasons why these things mentioned sometimes occur. Markets are often inaccessible, vegetables scarce and high, good cooks hard to procure, which spoil the best intentions of the most honest landlord.

Then there are a class of men who would grumble at the best dish that could possibly be served. They grumble when the coffee is hot, and when it is cold, drink six glasses of iced tea and complain when told it is out. They eat ham and eggs, beef-steak and grits, mutton chops and cold cabbage, light rolls and biscuits, batter-cakes and syrup—all for supper, get the colic in the night and then "cuss" the hotel man for *bad fare*. That's hardly *fair*.

I tell you, if hotel men get to heaven—and I hope they may—it will be through great trials and powerful tribulations. For they have been blessed out enough for tough beef, strong butter, blue-john milk, defunct ham, tainted mutton, short rations, that wonderful mystery—hash, "the substance of things hoped for, the evidence of things not seen," and high prices, till they can almost smell brimstone in their fly-specked dining-rooms.

The best thing a traveling man can do, is to be patient and kind in disposition, remembering that he did not have every thing he wanted while at home, and if he did, his home was not infested with the class of people hotel-men are constantly troubled with.

Speak kindly to every body—white and black, red and yellow, male and female, and Methodist preachers. You don't know when you will have need of one of them. The blackest negro boy that walks the streets may be the one who is to bring your water, black your boots, and serve your hash at meals at your hotel.

It always pays to introduce yourself plainly and affably, to the man with whom you expect to transact business. Always shake hands, that is, if he will allow you, for I remember to have introduced myself to a *man* in the beautiful city of Savannah, and extended my hand to get up a current of social intercourse. He recoiled from me like a humming-bird from a tom-cat. I recoiled too, and never sought his acquaintance further. He wasn't the man I was looking for.

A good, hearty shaking of the hand, though it be with an entire stranger, is a wonderful familiarizing medium. It brings the positive and negative together, and starts a current.

> "Give me the hand that is kind, warm and ready,
> Give me the clasp that is calm, true and steady;
> Give me the hand that will never deceive me,
> Give me its grasp, that I aye may believe thee.
> Soft is the palm of the delicate woman;
> Hard is the hand of the rough, sturdy yeoman;
> Soft palm or hard hand, it matters not—never!
> Give me the grasp that is friendly forever.
>
> "Give me the hand that is true as a brother;
> Give me the hand that has harmed not another;
> Give me the hand that has never forsworn it;
> Give me the grasp that I now may adorn it.
> Lovely the palm of the fair blue-veined maiden;
> Horny the hand of the workman o'erladen;
> Lovely or ugly, it matters not—never!
> Give me the grasp that is friendly forever."

Good clothes, pleasant manners, kind words and a bright, smiling face are worth more to a man who expects to spend his time on the road than titles or riches or an illustrious paternal ancestry. These won't do you much good when you wish to get the most out of human nature.

On the road! The very mention of it brings up in the memory many amusing incidents.

I was a general agent for Hitchcock's Analysis,

special agent for the Emory Mirror, *most especial* agent for the "Men and Women's Matrimonial Aid Association," and delegate to the State Sunday-school Convention, till you couldn't rest.

What a hobby I had on the Emory Mirror. Whenever I started out to get subscribers, what a time I had!

One bright spring evening, when the air was redolent with the perfume of peach blossoms, daisies and blue violets, and the birds and bees were kicking up generally about the beautiful weather that had so suddenly come, I started for Columbus to get *subscribers for the Mirror* (?)

The clouds had all departed, the mist and fog which had been hanging like a pall for so many long, weary days about the horizon had all departed. I took the train at four o'clock and by nightfall was in the Gate City.

Atlanta is a good place to pass through, no matter where you are bound. Always go through there if you want to have a good time on your trip. If you start out for a good time, perhaps you may not go any further.

One man is always as good as another, and sometimes better, in Atlanta, especially if he has money. Moreover, you will always pass for that you are worth there, if you aint worth much.

Well, I stood under the car shed that evening with about my usual degree of self-conceit, thinking perhaps I looked a little better than usual with my beaver, kid gloves and *tin-handled* cane on. Presently a very handsome gentleman, fully as good looking as myself stepped up to me and said,

"How do you do, Doctor?"

I bowed, extended my hand, and said,

"Are you not mistaken?"

"No, I guess not; aint this Doctor Westmoreland?"

Well, now, wasn't that a fix? I hated to deny the charge, yet was afraid to own it for fear the doctor would find it out, and then what?

"No, sir, S— from Emory College"—the next biggest thing I could acknowledge.

"Oh, a professor, I presume?"

Then the devil tempted me, for I was getting down to the bottom of things. I began to wish I had on an old slouch hat and a basket on my arm. I would have recognized the latter charge, but most of the professors were married and I feared their wives.

Then I commenced interrogating my new friend. I always talk to people who talk to me, and sometimes to those who don't seem inclined to talk.

"You're a member of the Atlanta bar?" said I.

"No," he replied, "I've just graduated at —— Medical College, north."

Ah! Jesso! He thought all men were doctors because he was one.

Then I concluded to act doctor and called around to see a young lady friend whom I hadn't seen in twelve months, to *inquire after her health*.

She came in the parlor looking as young and pretty as ever. I smiled and spoke poetically of the long days that had flown since we had last met—of sweethearts and flirtations—and I thought by her pleasant smiles that I was pleasing her wonderfully, when a gentleman passed the parlor door and I asked the *young lady* who that was.

"My husband—I've been married ten months."

"Ah hah! hem! Well—y-e-s! I–I believe I–hung my hat on the—the rack in the hall" (?)

I racked away, and the next subject I was studying was astronomy, as I turned the corner of the City Hall Park, all alone.

I went back to the car shed, took the Columbus-bound train, and lay down to dream of "It might have been"—but for another fellow.

When I arrived in Columbus a man stepped up to me and asked what it would cost him for *whatever* I might be representing. I told him *fifty cents*. He said "put me down for one," and asked in a kind of timid, modest way what it was. I told him the "Emory Mirror." He didn't open his mouth further. I had been there before.

When I returned to Oxford the editorial staff scored down about forty new subscribers, but I never told how much fun I had on that trip, which had been given me for the benefit of the paper.

During my college course the agency for the Emory Mirror afforded me more than a thousand miles ride, and much more experience as an agent, and lots of enjoyment. I went to Augusta, Savannah, Columbus, LaGrange, Cartersville and Atlanta, and received more than two hundred subscribers and one hundred dollars' worth of advertisements for the little college "Mirror."

Things moved on nicely in Virginia. Pauline's letters were all that anyone could wish. It was more of real business this time than a mere sickly sentimentality.

So many letters had been written in which the vows of love and the promises to be faithful had been repeated, that it seemed like a mockery to still dwell on them. It was more of the "when?" and "how?" and "where?" "Where shall we live and wherewithal shall we be clothed?" It takes a philosopher to answer these questions properly and satisfactorily. It remains to see whether I answered them satisfactorily to Pauline.

CHAPTER VII.

LIGHTS AND SHADOWS, OR, CONTRASTED PICTURES.

"As varied as the tinseling of a summer cloud; as variegated as the leaves of an autumnal forest, are the hues of human impulses and human feelings."

The sun rises in all its loveliness, adorns the world with garments of sparkling gold; paints each leaf a different dress; transforms every streamlet into a golden sash with which to wrap the world in beauty; crystalizes every dewdrop into a thousand sparkling gems, and sends joy and gladness singing their happy song of love around the world.

But ere it sinks to rest behind the western hills all is wrapped in thick clouds and dark shadows. The lightning flashes, the thunder roars, the howling storm plays its sad song among the trees, and nature drapes herself in mourning.

Thus it is with human hearts and human feelings. They present one continual panoramic view of joys and sorrows, hopes and fears, lights and shadows. We reach forth and pluck the brightest rose that blooms beside our pathway and feel with it its hidden thorns. We enjoy the richest fruits earth can yield and in them find the seeds that make a bitter taste.

We quaff the coolest draughts that sparkling founts distil and find in them a rude and unexpected chill.

The scene of human events is ever changing, leaving the mind to wonder what will next transpire.

I stood and gazed upon a beautiful human flower that played beside my pathway. I passed along and bowed to taste its sweet fragrance and view its beauty.

I passed again, and lo! it was gone. Its stem was leafless, its roots were withered, and the enclosure which surrounded it was broken down! I said,

> "Frail is our joys as is yon opening flower
> That spreads its fragrant blossom to the skies;
> Plucked by an intruder's hand, in one short hour
> Its bloom is withered and its fragrance dies."

How varied are the pictures of human nature which unfold themselves and show their beauty or their repugnance to him who would work his weary way through a college course by selling a book!

The world often looks down upon such a character with cold indifference, void of charity or sympathy. But everything has its advantages as well as its disadvantages, and there are some things to be learned, some profit to be derived, some pleasures to be enjoyed, some beautiful flowers to be culled, that could scarcely be attained in any other vocation in life.

For instance, had I never sold a book I might have lived and died without knowing hat a woman can sometimes really be at home when she is away.

"Missus tole me to tell ye she isn't at home."

I might never have known that many people do not buy books to read but only for the pictures, or because some one else has bought.

"Has your book any pictures in it?"

"No, madam."

"Well, then, I don't care for it."

"Did Col. Brown get one of your books, Mr. Special Agent?"

"No, sir."

"Well, I'll not take one to-day; I'll see you some other time." (After he sees Col. Brown.)

I might never have known that men sometimes tell the truth, and that women always do—sometimes, too.

I might never have observed how much good it does to tell a woman her baby is pretty.

"Oh, your child is so sweet, Mrs. Blizzard, it has such beautiful eyes. How sweet its disposition—really, it's the very image of its mother."

"Mr. S——, what did you say was the price of your book?"

"Ten dollars, madam."

"Well, I—I believe I'll take one. She will be large enough to read it after awhile. Oh, she's so sweet—te-tete-te!"

And I have really made so much of babies that I

have learned to love the little things, if they haint got sour milk on 'em.

Had I kept the even tenor of my way in the humbler walks of life, free from the jars and *bustles* that agitate the world, I might never have been ushered into elegant parlors draped with tapestry,

"Where the floor with tassels of fir is besprent
 Filling the room with their fragrant scent,"

ornamented with mirrors and oriental paintings, to find that the inmates were not able to buy a book.

I might never have discovered that very rich people never read; very poor people can't read, and that people in moderate circumstances always read and pay the preacher.

How different are individuals with whom we are daily coming in contact—each character presents a different shade in the portrait of human nature.

You have often seen a stereoscopic view of some principal street in a large city, taken instantaneously, what a picture it presents! Carriages, wagons, drays, buggies, 'busses, big wagons, little wagons, and dumping carts, bicycles, tricycles, and wheel-barrows, horses and mules, dogs and goats, men, women and children —black, white and yellow; sleek beavered fellows and poor, ragged beggars; cross-eyed, red-nosed men, freckle-faced, red-haired women; bright, glowing countenances, sad and despairing faces; the child of fashion in its elegant dress, and the "great unwashed" in its garments of dirt—some moving rapidly, others at a snail's gait; some going east, some going west, some north, some south—all toward the grave!

What a motley scene such a picture presents.

I have often thought, in looking upon such a scene, what a picture a photographed conversation would be to the mind's eye. To say the least of it, it would afford much material for thought.

Pass swiftly down the street, if you will, and catch, the different conversations and intonations as they fall from the lips of the busy world, and remember the different dispositions with which you daily come in contact and you can but say,

"Many men of many minds," many women of many fashions, many people of many passions, many drunkards of many drinks, many liars of many lies, many swearers of many swears.

One man says, "I wish it wasn't so hot." Another says, "I'm glad it's no hotter." One says, "I wish I had something better to eat." Another, "I'm glad I can get what I have."

"The rain will make mud," says one. Says another, "It will lay the dust."

One sighs "I wish I was dead." The other, "I am glad I am alive."

Everybody sees things from a different standpoint.

If you had heard a conversation which took place some time ago in one of our Southern cities, it would have run somewhat in this way:

"I'm a detective."

"Well, suppose you are."

"Aint you selling a book?"

"Yes, sir, you'd think so."

"Have you a license?"

"I have not; I don't use those things in this civilized country."

"Well, I guess you had better go with me and see about the matter.

"Well, my friend, you lay yourself liable to a fine of one hundred dollars or imprisonment."

I just walked down to the mayor's office and paid my twenty-five dollars without a word. I tell you it costs something to talk with everybody you meet— especially a detective. But then it pays too; business is business. I just went around and took in the mayor and aldermen—that's business.

"Mr., don't you want a hack?"

"No," said I, "I'm hacked now. Just paid twenty-five dollars for the privilege of talking. I'll hack somebody now."

"Mr., don't ye want me to cah'y yo valece down fur ye?"

"Down where?"

"Whah yere gwine."
"*Whah am I gwine?*"
"Dunno, sah!"
"Well, I'm going to talk a man to death; the funeral won't take place till to-morrow."

The scene is ever changing. In the same city the electric lights had created quite a sensation. They were beautiful things. You could see them just as plain, if you were close enough and the moon shone bright—the glass globes, you know.

Passing up Bull street one evening, just as I approached one of the towers, I saw a colored man standing on the sidewalk with hands up and eyes big as saucers. I said,

"Uncle, how about it?"

"Boss, I'ze shame to own it, sah, but clar fo' God, I'ze bin livin' heah fifteen years, an' I'se jist bin outen de city fo' a fu daiz and when I kempt inter town dis eben it wah fifteen minits fo' I node whah I is. Daze liten up dem upper rejuns—an' I'ze gwine dat way, sho'. Yes, sah, I is."

I rang the silver door-bell of a brown stone front not long since, and a servant came to the door; I handed her my card and asked if I could see Mrs. Bonton. The servant went back, and through the long hall I could hear the conversation:

"Gemmen to de do'."

"How's he dressed?"
"Very well, mum."
"What's he got?"
"A police, mum."
"Guess he's a tinker. Tell him I don't want anything mended to-day. Can't see him to-day nor to-morrow either."

I received the intelligence and passed down town thinking,

"There's never a cup so pleasant
But has bitter with the sweet;
There's never a path so rugged
That bears not the print of feet;
And we have a helper promised
For the trials we may meet.

"There's never a garden growing
With roses in every plot;
There's never a heart so hardened
But has its tender spot;
We have only to prune the border
To find the touch-me-not."

Passing further down the street, I pulled the string to another bell. The servant came to the door, I handed her my card, and through the hall the sound came,

"Mr. S——, from Emory College. Ask him in the parlor and give him a fan; bring in some fresh water and tell him I'll be there in a few minutes."

"Howdy do, Mr. S——; you're a student at Emory?"

"Yes, madam, and canvassing, during my vacation to get ready, financially, to go back to college. I'll show you my work."

"Certainly, sir; I'll look at it with pleasure. My husband and two brothers graduated there, and I am interested in all her interests."

I showed it to her in first-class style, and she said,

"I'll take it. Come to see me, Mr. S——, while you're in the city."

"Thank you, madam."

And I went off singing,

>"There's never a way so narrow
>But the entrance is made straight;
>There's always a guide to point us
>To the little wicket gate;
>And the angels will be nearer
>To a soul that is desolate."

While in Macon, I sat one evening in an office talking to a young man, well educated, of handsome physique, attractive manners, and attractive withal. He was waiting for the wheel of fortune to turn round and reveal some streak of luck, I waiting for the clouds to pass off that I might make a streak.

We talked of the past, with its disappointments of love as well as in fortune; of the girls we had courted, tried to flirt with and got "kicked;" of the future, with its hopes and prospects of success.

Presently the clouds parted, the sun broke forth in

its accustomed beauty, and the delightful evening addressed itself to the active mind of the business man. I said,

"Good-bye, Frank, there are forts in this town that have not been stormed, as yet, and success is only to the persevering."

"Stay longer," cried Frank; "the day is far spent and you can do but little between this and night."

But I turned away from Frank and said to myself, as I picked up my valise,

"Where thou goest, there will I not go, and where thou diest, there will I not be buried."

As I passed down Poplar street I cast my eyes up at the old city clock that stands there day after day, making fun of idlers, and saw that the hand pointed to four o'clock. But that evening at twilight when I counted up my profits I found I had made fifteen dollars and nobody hurt—I was glad I was not hurt.

Many young men forego the privilege of doing something for fear they will fail. The best thing a Chinaman ever said was that "our greatest glory was not so much in *not failing*, but in knowing how to *rise* out of a failure."

There are so many lights and shadows which make up the portrait of human nature, that one dodging in and out at intervals, and seeing nothing but the heavier dark lines, concludes that really it is an unsightly scene; and indeed you often have some grounds for thinking so. One is often discouraged in fighting the battle of life because he meets so much opposition. Some people are so crabbed, so uncouth, that really we sometimes wish that we had never entered the race and assumed the responsibilities that come in the business transactions of—well, say a special agent."

For example, I stepped up on the portico of an elegant mansion in one of our Southern cities some time ago, rang the bell, sent my card in, and was presently ushered into a handsome parlor.

The lady of the house entered in a few moments, elegantly dressed, wearing the smile of a saint, and addressed me in tones soft and musical.

I rose, bowed and said,

"This is Mrs. Wealthy, I presume."

"Yes, sir; keep your seat."

"I am a student at Emory College, and during my vacation am representing a very fine work, which I shall take great pleasure in showing you."

"Certainly, sir, I shall look at your work with delight."

In the most fascinating style I showed the work, revealing beauty after beauty, until the good lady was entirely enraptured with the work. She took her own lily-white hand and wrote her name in my order book—her own sweet little name. I bowed, and telling her I would be on hand about the twenty-fifth of the month, I departed. As I went off down town I thought of what an angel I had met.

I ordered the book, paying for it, the freight, boxing and carting, and drayage, and on the day the order was due I tripped lightly up the steps, rang the bell, and announced my arrival with the book.

"I believe I don't want the book; I've changed my mind."

"But, madam, I've ordered the book, and shall expect you to take it, according to contract."

"Yes; but I didn't say I would take it."

"I beg your pardon, madam, but I have your name in your own handwriting."

That good (?) *woman* turned around, and, calling her husband (a man with whom I was not acquainted, and one whose looks were not such as to prepossess one in his favor) said,

"This man has disputed my word!" (My own, sweet little word.)

Then that man! why he swelled up like a toad and looked as red as a turkey gobbler's snout, and doubled up his fists and looked at me—well, I hardly know how he did look, for I didn't stay long enough to see how he appeared. He said,

"I'll shake your head off your shoulders if you dispute my wife's word!"

And that sweet-spirited angel stood there and said, "Sic him, Tige!" Then I said,

"My dear sir, if you do not want this beautiful book I will take it down the street to a man who wants it worse than you do—and I won't be long about it."

"I don't care where you take it just so you don't dispute my wife's word!"

Well, I skipped on the theory that "if 'twere well done when 'tis done, then 'twere well 'twere done quickly."

As I passed down the street I said to myself, "More folks have angels besides God."

That's about as dark shading as the artist generally puts into a picture unless he were painting a regular "hog-killing" time. But there is many a beautiful, green oasis in the desert of a *book agent's* life.

For example, in the suburbs of our own Southern cities, near the crumbling ruins of an old college, stands a faded dwelling. The magnolias, cape jasmines and cedar trees that stand in the yard, the half-dilapidated lattice fence encircling the foregrounds, the curved walk that leads up to the house, all tell of a once beautiful home.

I stopped my buggy, and tying the horse, I entered the half-open gate swung back on its rusty hinges, and started up the walk. Not a footprint could be seen on the white sand that lay in the path. The autumn leaves lay crisp and colored with many a hue in the mellow light of the fall day.

The undisturbed spider had woven his silken web from one column to the other with many an interlacing thread. As I walked up on the porch a hollow echo greeted my ears as though the feet that trod these planks made never a sound.

As I touched the knob of the door-bell it almost seemed as though I had hold of the bell that would wake the spirits from their sleeping place! As I turned the handle it screamed and grated in its rusty socket, and the dull, heavy twang that rang out rebounded against the bare walls within. This was all I could hear, and I turned to walk away, saying lightly to myself, "surely no one has been here in months."

But I chanced to mention to a passer-by that the lady was not at home up in the grove.

"Oh yes," said he, "you don't know how to enter. Go back, and when you pass through the gate turn to the left and follow the path that leads round to the rear of the house; there you will find a bell tied with a chain, ring that and go back to the front door."

I did so, and the servant met me and conducted me into the sitting-room.

There was an air of departed spirits and former glory, that marked every thing upon which I looked.

I felt a strange sensation, such as one would expect to feel on entering the abode of a hermit.

A door opened and in walked a rather tall female form, of delicate, but very graceful proportions. The dark brown, glossy hair already intermingled with threads of gray; the heavy eye-brows and long, dark lashes; the round, hazel eye, beginning to sink with age, and the symmetrical features of a calm, but thoughtful face, already plowed in furrows of sorrow and care, marked the *physique* of a once beautiful woman.

I felt that I stood in the presence of one of God's chosen saints.

I introduced myself and business, and told her the purpose for which I was thus laboring. She encouraged me by taking my work and giving many words of cheer. Her life of sorrow had made her so sympathetic.

I said to myself as I went away, " Yes, your life of sorrow has ' worked out for you a far more exceeding and eternal weight of glory,' and you are the sweetest Christian spirit I ever saw !"

I went away from that house a better and a happier boy, thinking how little of fashion and show it took to make the purest, happiest Christian the world ever knew!

When I came around later in the season to deliver

her the work, she paid me for it and made me accept a note besides in token of her appreciation of my undertaking. Thus it was by being richer, wiser, and better, I thanked God and took courage.

It is in the beautiful month of October, the heated vacation with its arduous labors is over, eighteen hundred dollars worth of books have been sold and delivered, within the short space of ninety days. Autumn has already thrown its enchanting witchery over the scene. The sylvan village of Oxford is all astir with the arrival of old and new students coming in for the opening of the fall term.

Old friends, class-mates, room-mates and new faces, all meet in the classic grove under the shadows of the broad-spreading oaks, and of Seney Hall, which has grown to completion during the absence of the students.

The senior class meet for their last autumnal term. They will never again come together under these shady oaks in this capacity, and doubtless, if ever, in any other—some will be missing.

It is a joyous time to many happy hearts. To some, the scenes that surround them, and the bright smiles and joyous laughter are all new and novel—to others, it is merely a repetition of the delights of a college life.

As the western sun gilds the fields and campus

oaks, and robes them in garments of a myriad tints, a dozen groups of students can be seen standing here and there in the shadows that are fast lengthening, some busily engaged in the business of secret society matters, others discussing the pleasures of the past and prospects for the future.

The mosquito plays around the end of one's nose as though he wished to be happy, too, and form some kind of *secret society* alliance with the brotherhood of man.

The mocking bird is trilling its last sweet notes as the bright day dies away into soft fairy-like twilight.

The lamp lights are beginning to glow from the kitchen and dining-room windows of the boarding houses. The soft zephyrs steal gently up from the ocean through the dark green foliage and mingle with the happy laughter of the dispersing groups. A few linger on the steps of Seney Hall, just under the old clock that peals forth its sonorous music every thirty minutes.

These are friends, members of a mystical brotherhood, bound together by ties of love and affection. Each is inquiring after the happiness and prosperity of the others.

G.—" Well, S——, what has been your success financially this vacation ?"

S.—" The best I ever had, thank you."

H.—" S——, how much did you really make ?"

S.—" I don't know exactly—I know I did well and had a good time besides."

T.—" Say, old fellow, how about your White Oak Camp-meeting sweetheart ?"

S.—"Oh, she busted me."

H.—"How about your Atlanta girl ?"

S.—"She played the wild with me, too."

All.—"Ha! ha! ha!"

C.—"What of your Milledgeville girl ?"

S.—"She busted me too."

"Well, say, S.," said G.—who seemed to have the inside track on matters—"how about your Virginia sweet-heart? How has that turned out? Miss Pauline, you know?"

S.—"Well, boys, I'll tell you what it is, as it's all in the family and will not go any further, the way things stand now I'm busted all round. I received a letter from Pauline the other day which ruins my hopes with her."

H.—"What's the matter there now, S. ?"

S.—"Why, boys, you see Pauline is a proud, high-minded woman, raised in luxury, has had all that heart could wish, and however much she cares for me she don't like my prospects for the future.

"You see the ministry, so far as this world's goods go, is not an easy life, and this is the rock which has scattered my hopes with Pauline.

"I wouldn't give up my purposes and honest convictions of right for the best woman in the world. She tells me," concluded S., "that 'she had hoped I would at least make my home in Virginia, and have a nice little home near her parents.' But that if I 'expected to remain in Georgia, and drag her around from pillar to post, that the matter is ended.'

"I guess it is all up, for I expect to remain right here and fight it out on the line of duty. It will be all the better for me, though, as I will have nothing to bother me during this, my last year in college, and I can make good use of my time. I shall swing out as free from the influence of woman as a balloon a mile high in the etherial regions."

As these club-mates strolled down through the campus toward Marvin Hall, they sang—

>Roll on, O calm and peaceful night,
>   Complete thy round of star-lit splendor;
>Burst the golden gates with light,
>   Let richer, broader glory tend her.
>
>And as thy soft and mellow light
>   Will not think to wane nor vanish,
>But rise to bright effulgence height,
>   And never with the evening tarnish,
>
>So may our brightest cherished dreams
>   Bud forth and bloom and blossom,
>Till each his laden vineyard gleams
>   And feasts on richest fruit—Opossum!

CHAPTER VIII.

FINALE.

The snow is falling rapidly. The cold December winds are hurling and dashing the white flakes through the leafless trees of the campus oaks at whistling speed.

The clouds are dark and lowering. The soft white fleece that covers the ground cracks and pops under the feet of the college student as he plods his way from his warm room to answer the ring of the two o'clock bell Friday evening.

It is on the eve of Christmas. Some of the students have been from home longer since the opening of fall term than ever before. Three short months seem to them an age, while others have not darkened the door of the parental roof in four long years.

Snowballs fly promiscuously, one occasionally grazing the head of a professor as he hurries toward his recitation-room. The merry laugh of the student rings out on the campus in all directions. A spirit of joyous, innocent rebellion pervades every heart.

"We must have an extra holiday or we'll all run off," was the cry from fifty noisy voices. Two dozen students enter the president's office requesting permission to leave on the four o'clock train for Atlanta and home. The kind heart of the president is touched, and when the train rolls into the little station at Midway, twenty boys board the train for the "*Gate City!*"

It is a jolly crowd, and while it is not a boisterous, drinking party (for they were gentlemen) still there is much hilarity, mingled with wit and humor, that would make a passenger occasionally smile despite his intentions to be dignified. Dyspepsia and saturninity " hide out" when a score of college boys get together on a railroad train.

Approaching one of the stations on the road the wit said:

" We are approaching that station whose characteristic productions are those caciferous and ovicular receptacles of gallinaceous vitality which, after passing through a certain form of culinary art are known as "*biled eggs*." Then, pulling out a handful of cigars, he soliloquized on this wise:

" We will now regale ourselves with a few of the monocotyledonous, endogenous phenogams known under the technical name of *nicotina tobaccum*. The highest form resulting from the evolution of this plant is somewhat cylindrical in shape, slender in form, slightly convex at one extremity, and is recognized by its generally carrying some *dude* around who swings to one end of it."

Thus they remarked the whole way, keeping the car in a roar of laughter throughout the journey.

Some of the students concluded to remain over during the night and take in the beautiful mud that had congregated itself *en masse* throughout the city.

The mud was really a sight to see. Why, it was three miles wide, and extended from Ponce de Leon clear to West End, and from the cemetery to the Rolling Mills. The "beautiful snow" had filled the ground below, and had been ground and mixed by the wheels of buggies, wagons, drays, dumping carts, bicycles, tricycles, wheelbarrows, and by the feet of men, women and children, horses and mules and dogs, until it had lost its virgin whiteness and poetic beauty.

But mud did not keep the people from going in Atlanta. No, everybody goes, men, women, boys, girls, preachers, sisters of charity, brothers of charity, newsboys, bootblacks, white boys, black boys, and— mud.

Yes, they all go. Young ladies just tuck up their dresses, and pull their veils over their faces, so they can't see, and just go! go! go! The people here are like Longfellow's Mad River, for

"They go on forever!"

There is a great deal to see in Atlanta about Christmas times. For instance, there is the tin horn, and the red wagon, and the—the mud! and there is the well-dressed man, and the man with the red nose and the muddy coat.

Then, above all, and beneath all, and over all is the —mud!

Well, some of the boys concluded they could not take in everything in one short evening, so they would remain over night.

"Where would be a good place to stay?" asked several boys, including the wit and the parson.

"At 61 Marietta street," was the reply.

"Very good," said the parson; "I may not get in until late, as I expect to call on a lady friend of mine, but I guess there'll be no trouble in finding the room where the students are stored away."

So about ten o'clock p. m. the wit found he had seen enough of the town, and coming up to the gate that led into a little yard in front of 61, he found it fastened.

"What shall I do?" soliloquized the wit. "I can jump the fence, but I'm afraid of dogs."

So he took his beaver off and laid it down carefully and jumped the palings to see if the coast was clear. Finding everything all right and "quiet along the Potomac," he jumped back for his hat. He placed the beaver upon his head and with his supple limbs he lit over again with all ease; but the beaver didn't follow. It lit on the same side as that from which it started. Then he jumped back again, and placing it more tightly on his cranium, made his final leap and reached his room in safety. He had graduated in gymnastics or he never would have gotten in at No. 61.

But ah! the parson—his time came next. He had gone a dozen blocks out Whitehall street to see his lady friend, and her company was so delightful that the hour of twelve had arrived before he thought of leaving.

But bidding his lady-love *good-bye*, and wishing her a "Happy New Year" a dozen times, he started for 61 Marietta. But alas! alas! not so easily found. He went to the first corner and turned to the right, to the next corner and turned to the left, to the third corner and turned to the right, and thus he wandered from one square to another, until the lights in the dwellings began to grow scarce, but no nearer his goal than when he had first left his lady love's residence.

Round and round he went, and finally coming to a residence where a light glowed from the window, faint and weary with his unsuccessful wanderings, he stepped up on the portico and rang the bell.

Several little children ran to the door and the parson said—

"Children, who lives here?"

Then the children laughed right out in his face.

"Children, can you tell me the way to the Kimball House?"

Then the children laughed louder and ran back into the room.

"What can this mean?" muttered the parson.

Then a young lady came to the door and said,

"W-e-l-l, Mr. L——, where have you been?"

And the parson said,

"W-e-l-l, Miss Fannie, is this your house?"

The poor fellow had walked two miles right round his sweetheart's home and had called an hour later to know his way to the Kimball House.

She gladly directed him to the proper street that would lead him down town. The parson reached the boarding-house safely, tripped lightly up stairs and entered a room to the right. An alto voice said,

"Who's that?"

"It's one of the students. I wish to retire."

"Well, *retire* out of here as quickly as you can—oh, me! my! oh!"

Then turning to the left he entered another room, and the bass voice of some clerk said,

"Who's that?"

"It's me. I'm hunting the students."

"Well, the students are down stairs."

Then the parson went down stairs and turned to the left, and a sweet little soprano voice said:

"Who's that?—O!"

"It's me. I'm hunting the students."

"Well, they are on the other side of the hall."

Then the parson turned to the right, half scared to death, and one of the boys says he was as white as a sheet, when he found the right room.

The parson has been west since that time, but has never been necessitated to have his girl show him the way home, nor jump the fence to get in the yard, nor wake up all the sweet little angels at his boarding-house hunting the students, since that eventful night in the Gate City.

Christmas day had arrived. Three o'clock Monday evening the State Road train pulled from under the car-shed northward. A few short stops along the line to allow passengers to get on and off, and I arrived at the station nearest the residence of Rosa Hawthorne.

Rosa and I had met in Atlanta during the fall and had made up again. I had been invited to spend Christmas at her home, some miles out from the Gate City.

Procuring a horse and buggy at the little village where I left the railroad, I proceeded in the direction of Rosa's country home.

It was a damp, muddy, drizzly evening. The horse dashed and splashed along over the red clay hills, while phantoms and visions and air-castles appeared and disappeared in quick succession in my busy brain.

The evening is waning, the clouds are dark and heavy, the mist and fog gather close in front of the steaming steed. It is a time for reflection, the sun has hid himself behind a heavy vail of December clouds and mist. The flowers that would on some spring evening call forth delightful thoughts, are hid beneath the mud and snow of a dark winter day ; the birds that would sing a sweet song to the rolling wheels of a vehicle over a smooth road in summer, have flown to a more genial clime ; the mind is necessarily shut up to itself, memories of the past intrude themselves upon us, our thoughts go back over the past, the scenes of other days rise to the retrospective gaze, the sweetest and saddest memories of life steal in upon us, the days of our youth, the friends we have loved and lost, the hopes we have cherished—all are reviewed with the freshness of yesterday.

It is not alone with the past that thought is engaged in such an hour ; it projects itself into the future, searching amid the years that are to come for what of joy or sorrow they have in store for us. "Alas! we have here no abiding home, the sands beneath our feet are constantly washed by the inflowing tide of ceaseless years ; soon, and inevitably the objects of our affections shall be taken from us, or we be taken from them." How shall we successfully meet the responsibilities that await us? What steps are necessary to carry forward the schemes which minister comfort in the line of duty? These are the questions which imperatively demand consideration.

Rosa had invited me to enjoy the hospitalities of her happy home, made more happy on this special occasion by a delightful Christmas party.

The prospects for the future with Rosa must now be decided. The day for our happy union must be fixed and proper steps taken for its consummation.

Years have gone by since I first left home, and but one visit made to the parental roof in all that time; and to graduate six months hence, marry, and go back to Virginia with a sweet bride, would be the crowning period of my life.

Will time throw no shadow over these bright dreams? God only knows!

On the foaming steed pushes; the white-capped peaks of the Blue Ridge, in the far Northwestern portion of Georgia, are dimly seen above the fog that settles low to the cold, damp earth.

A mile in the distance is a lovely country residence, situated on a considerable eminence, skirted by a winding stream that steals down from the mountains of North Georgia. Hill after hill, forest after forest rise beyond and are lost in the unbroken chain of circling mountains. An orchard, a well filled barn and cribs, together with the residence before mentioned, crown the eminence which overlooks the surrounding country.

The dark shadows are fast gathering; the big log fires begin to send forth their light from country dwellings as I pass them in quick succession; the light in the parlor on the hill shines with an inviting gleam.

Carriages and buggies dash up and unload their contents until soon the house is all astir with the happy voices of cheerful men and maidens.

Music and merry song and innocent games and an elegant supper wore this Christmas evening away into the short hours. A few hurried sentences from Rosa, amid the buzz and the stir of the evening, revealed to my anxious heart the desired fact that all was well.

"Rosa, but six short months intervene between this and the glad day of my graduation, and our happy marriage. With what I have made and saved through economy from my expenses in college, I feel justified in starting out on the delightful sea of matrimony. Soon my college expenses will no longer drain my treasury, and to enter upon my mission in life with such a companion as you, will prove, indeed, a mission of love."

"All your joys and sorrows it will be the delight of my life to share. My prayer is that nothing may intervene to thwart our purpose and becloud the bright days of our future."

With such an assurance, the day or two at Rosa's country home, away from books and college classes, was delightfully enjoyed.

Back again at the railroad, a few hours' ride, with one change of cars, and the train blows for Covington.

It is the silent hour of midnight. Nothing can be heard about the quiet village of Oxford but the familiar bark of the cur as he marks the returning student steal in from his Christmas dissipations.

A myriad sparkling worlds have marshaled in the deep firmament above. The white snow has all gone except here and there a white spot, reminding one of a picnic in a grove with the table cloths spread under the broad oaks.

I enter the portico of Marvin Hall, thrust my hand into a letter box containing the accumulated mail, strike a match and find a half dozen letters awaiting my arrival. I enter my room, and those known to be business letters are hurriedly opened and the contents quickly noted.

There remains one small, white envelope neatly addressed in a lady's hand.

"This will be a treat, I know," I remarked to myself, recognizing my sister's writing on the superscription. I tore it open and began reading.

But alas! alas! The old year may hold in its embrace the happiest heart that ever fluttered in a human breast! and the new year sing the sad requiem over the departed hopes of one's brightest and most cherished imaginations.

"M——, Dec. —, 188 .

" Dear Brother :

"This morning the sun rose beautifully upon our peaceful and happy home; to-night it sinks to rest upon its smouldering and crumbling ruins! * * *

Your affectionate sister,

Fannie."

Oh, God! my home! the home of my youth, with its sweet clustering memories—my home all in ashes!

Alas! Whatever may be our home, rudely or tastefully constructed ; whether it be the humble hut or the stately mansion, with marble steps and gilded halls, and spacious apartments hung with richest tapestry, in the quiet of the country or in the bustle of the crowded city, we build and garnish, knowing that it is doomed to loss or to decay.

Unnumbered forces work its destruction. The crackling flames may devour it, the tornado may scatter it to the winds, the earthquake may upheave it to its foundations, the slow, tedious attritions of years may crumble it to the dust; an unforeseen calamity may wrench it from our grasp, still the loss (come when or how it may) to us can never be computed.

It was something more than so much brick and mortar and timber. It was the center of a thousand hallowed recollections. From basement to garret there was not a room or a spot but was dear to memory, because of the associations that clustered about it.

Perhaps it was the old homestead of the family, or perchance the purchase of hard-earned money by some emigrant who went out West. But no matter for that. It has a hold upon our affections, and if our life has been spent there, we can scarely look back to it except through tears.

A host of shadowy recollections crowd upon us, some bright, some sad. Our infancy may have been hushed to rest beneath its roof by the loving voice of a tender mother.

The joys and grief of childhood, the hopes of budding manhood or womanhood are inseparably connected with its enclosures. Beneath the blooming trellis at the door, when the moonbeams crept through the mantling vines, the vows of love were breathed.

A thousand memories are awakened by the retrospective gaze, each in turn making the thoughts of home more sacred.

The wreck comes—a financial disaster, a fire, the corroding touch of time, and what is the loss? A stranger comforts us with these words, "It is a trifle; it can easily be replaced." Never, never! He knows not how much more than that which is seen has been hopelessly shivered or lies buried beneath the smouldering ruins. A more elegant mansion may grow up in the place of the old; more beautiful and tasteful grounds may be planned; the birds may come back in the springtime as of yore and build their nests under the roof; others may admire it; but to us it is not the home in which we were born and reared; the associations are gone, the spell is broken, the charm is lost. We are strangers beneath our own roof.

Such were my thoughts as I stood speechless and in tears, with this little note in my cold fingers.

But this was not all. A voice of duty speaks again—

"What have you ever done for your parents?"

"Not much, if anything."

"Is not this a time to help?"

The heart could but answer, "Yes!"

Then comes a struggle. How can I leave my class whom I love so much, and forego the pleasure of graduating with them? They never seemed half so dear to me before. We have been together several years; our hopes and our prospects for the future are to a great degree bound together, and now the voice of duty says these pleasant associations must now come to an end. The future which but a moment ago seemed so bright, is now all dark and unproductive of the happiness I had expected.

Eighteen months must of necessity pass now before my graduation day, and the other pleasant expectations realized.

Still another thought comes dashing into the already fevered brain. When I tell Rosa that I shall leave college and go out to repair the damages of the flames, will she agree to wait? Ah! me! this would have been a time to have said,

"I'll not finish my education, the road is too rough."

But thank God, a little voice whispered through the darkness and broke the stillness of this silent midnight hour, in words like these,

> Though every joy may foam
> On the bosom of many years,
> Still never a foam brings a brave bark home—
> It reaches the haven through tears.

And through tears and sorrow I saw into the future—a light falling on the path of duty, that gave me courage to sacrifice the little buds which seemed to be just about to open into the full blown flower of perfect happiness.

Kind Providence always designs rightly and well

for his children when they obey His will, and let come what may, one is always safe in placing his hand in God's and being led by him through the rough places in life. I carried the matter to Him and next morning, while my heart was still sad at the thoughts of my parents' inconvenience caused by this untimely calamity, my mind was made up as to the right course to pursue.

"I will leave college and go out to talk my way over a book and help repair damages, let the consequences be as they may."

I indited a short note to Rosa, telling her of the necessity of leaving college, and asking her to allow me to postpone our marriage a year longer than we had expected. I trembled with anxiety in waiting for a reply to this request.

In the meantime I made the necessary arrangements for leaving, sold my large arm rocking chair, student's lamp, bedstead and bed-clothes, table and cover, carpet and curtains, and began to say good-bye.

It was one of the trying hours of my life. "Good-bye Harry and George, Ed. and Bartow, Will and Carvey, farewell all! I had expected to have the pleasure of going to Atlanta to have our pictures taken, but I'll not be there! I had almost made my engagement for the senior party, but I'll be far away when that delightful occasion takes place.

"Good-bye Rosa. If you refuse to wait—well, I must go."

Will I be successful financially, finish my course, claim the hand of Rosa Hawthorne, and go home on a visit to see my loved ones, as I had so recently fancied I would?

A letter from New York city making me general agent for Hitchcock's Analysis, my trunk packed, a short sympathetic note from Rosa saying that no such trivial affair as a little time should come between us and separate us forever; a few hurried good-byes and I was off on the road again.

The first place I stopped was at Savannah. Fifteen hundred dollars worth of books sold and delivered there in ninety days, and I moved further south; Brunswick, St. Simon's Island, and Darien, were no less productive of success.

Much of pleasure may be mixed up with a business like this, that amply repays one for all the rebuffs he may receive from the rough and uncouth.

It was while in Brunswick, that I enjoyed the delightful pleasure of a fishing party which will haunt me with pleasant memories when the trials of *book agencies* will have been forgotten.

One beautiful May morning, just as the sun marked out a sparkling belt of glittering gold as he tinged each ripple of the water in his path from the wharf eastward, and the gentle zephyrs fanned from the brow the pestiferous "sand-fly gnat," two ladies and two gentlemen, one of the latter being myself, stepped aboard a little " gull," and turning its bow towards the Island of St. Simon's, we shot like a silver fish over the rippling tide as sweetly and as gently as an infant's breath.

But an hour's ride, and we had left the busy city far behind us, buried in the thick foliage of the water oak and elm, trimmed in their long, lacy robes of gray moss.

I had heard much of the rolling deep, and of "gathering up shells by the sea shore," but not till then, on that glad day, did I realize what it was to stroll for miles along the singing, rolling, ever restless tide, on the solid white sand, washed and rolled and lashed into snowy whiteness by the coming and the going of these untiring waves.

As I sat on an old battered boat, drifted and halfburied in the sand, and looked as far as the eye could reach at the white-capped waves as they rose and fell, and heard the deep-toned bass of this grand music, I read another chapter from the book of nature in which I saw more plainly than ever the sentence, "There is a God!"

God has revealed himself in every leaf and fruit and flower and grain of sand and drop of water, and towering mountain and stretching valley, and winding stream and sparkling sunbeam and twinkling star; but nowhere does "nature's God" speak so loudly and so plainly as in the ceaseless, billowing deep!

Back to Brunswick, business completed, and off to the "vine-clad hills" of Valdosta and Quitman. Here is where the *water-millions* and "cukes" grow.

When the mosquitoes and the rays of the Southern sun became too numerous, I sought the hills of North Georgia. Washington, Sparta, Athens and other places successfully canvassed, and autumn comes again. The Northeastern railroad, leading out from Athens, stops at Tallulah Falls. Why not visit this delightful place and study the beauties of nature instead of relying entirely on text-books and history?

The last days of beautiful September are quietly stealing away, penciling the leaves of the forest oak with their autumnal brush. The hazy *Indian veil* drapes itself in blue and purple folds along the sides of the mountain slopes with a fairy-like delicateness. Forest after forest, mountain peak after mountain peak rise and are lost in the blue distance beyond! The engine puffs and blows up the steep grade, leaving the plains and valleys far below. At midnight the Air-Line train halts for a moment, trembles as its mighty pulse throbs and beats, and an Emory College student lands high and dry in the lovely little city of Toccoa.

In such a climate as this one "draws the drapery of his couch about him and lies down to pleasant dreams" without the interruptions of either sand-fly or mosquito.

Day dawns. The sun rises and gilds the mountain peaks with a thousand variegated hues! The soft zephyrs steal up from the mountain gorges and whisper a sweet song to the opening autumnal day.

We leave the little city of Toccoa and gradually descend for a mile to the valley that lies beneath the overhanging precipice. We steal quietly up through the densely shaded glen, lighted only by the soft morning light that filters through the autumn leaves of the forest oak.

How easily one breathes in such an atmosphere! How subdued and reverential are the feelings as one approaches such divine architecture that is so soon to be revealed to the anxious eye! Ho! what music is this we hear as it is borne away on the mountain breeze?

Eternal architect! Thou hast clothed this mountain-bride with a flowing veil of sparkling water. Above, it hangs for a moment, rippling over the face of the mighty rock, then unfolds and drapes itself at the foot in clouds of mist and silvery spray.

How I Got My Education.

Toccoa is the beautiful bride adorned for her husband, standing in the mountain gorge, singing her sweet song as she awaits the approach of her husband. But, alas! Tallulah, though only sixteen miles distant, never approaches nearer.

I ascended to the top, took off my shoes and waded out into the center of the stream where the beautiful Indian maiden stood for the last time on earth. As I peeped over the mighty precipice this sweet song floated back from the murmuring waters below, and the soul experienced that deep and exquisite sense of the beautiful which is reserved for such moments to be enjoyed:

> Beautiful brook! when the moonlight's gleam
> Glistens upon thy falling stream,
> And the varied tints of thy rainbow vie
> With the brightest hues of the evening sky,
> The woodland elf and the merry fay
> Chat on thy banks their roundelay;
> And with fairy sword and tiny spear
> Fight o'er their bloodless battles here
> The drowsy bird from its leafy nook
> Peers on the whole with anxious look
> And the cricket uplifteth its cheerful voice
> And the bats at the merry sound rejoice,
> And the fairy troop on their sylvan green,
> Frolic and dance in the moonlight's sheen.
>
> Who would not leave Ambition's dream
> To linger here by the crystal stream?
> Or turn him from Fame's trumpet call
> To the softer sound of thy waterfall,

> And free from the toils and pangs of strife
> Pass the glad hours of his peaceful life?
> Nature no fairer knights doth rear
> Than those which gladden the vision here;
> And never yet did sunlight shine
> On sweeter vale and plain than thine.
>
> Beautiful streamlet! onward glide,
> In thy destined course to the ocean's tide!
> So youth impetuous longs to be
> Tossed on the waves of manhood's sea;
> But weary soon of the cloud and blast,
> Sighs for the haven its bark hath past:
> And though thou rushest now with glee,
> By hill and plain to seek the sea,
> No lovelier spot again thou'lt find
> Than that thou leavest here behind;
> Where hill and rock "rebound the call"
> Of clear Toccoa's waterfall!

As I turned and rode away from this incarnation of the beautiful, my soul, silent and speechless, could but unconsciously whisper "There is a God!"

Back to the city of Toccoa and then on to Tallulah. Arriving there, dinner over, a long walking stick in hand, and I began to *descend downward*, and down and down I went for about a thousand feet!

The water's edge is reached and one is instantly struck with the contrast between this and the beautiful Toccoa. Here is experienced the deepest sense of *grandeur!* What a wild, weird look lurks about the dark craggy granite and the white foaming waters! How the stream boils and seethes and lashes its impenetrable bed, as it leaps from one precipice to another!

The hand of nature has turned its course and forever shut it in between the towering walls of this "Grand Chasm." The sound that reaches the ear of the tourist from some eminence like the Devil's Pulpit, is a deep, solemn requiem-like music.

One is awed into silence and deep reverence, such as the heart could seldom feel under any other circumstances, as he stands in the presence of "Tempestuous," "Hurricane" and "Oceana," and looks up whence they make their mighty leap, then far above and beyond, block after block of dark granite is piled till it rears its august head almost out of sight.

These falls must be seen to be appreciated. No writer's pen or painter's brush can portray to the eye or mind what God has revealed in this, his mighty handiwork.

It is dangerous to visit a bar-room before starting out on this journey, for steady nerves and strong muscles are required to visit the different points of interest along the edge of the chasm, or to scramble down its steep and rugged face to behold the mad struggles of the troubled river:

> A mountain torrent I have seen,
> Where skies are bright and woods are green;
> A mountain river, rushing on
> Betwixt eternal walls of stone,

Down in a deep and dark abyss,
Bedded with rock and precipice;
Now, flowing with a sullen course
And uttering murmurs loud and hoarse,
Now, plunging with resistless tide
Adown a precipice's side;
Enwrapped in snowy foam and spray
It thunders on its headlong way,
Till mingled with the flood below
It there resumes its wonted flow.
Again, and yet again it leaps
From base to base—down rocky steeps;
Rending the air with ceaseless roar,
Swelled by loud echoes from each shore;
Beauty and grandeur there combine
And o'er the varied landscape shine,
There are a thousand charms displayed
Of rock and stream and hill and glade.
Tallulah claims the poet's lay,
This humble tribute song I pay.

Leaving Tallulah I found myself back at Athens, preparatory to starting for South Georgia, as had only six more months in college, my presence was not needed there till spring term.

So coming by Oxford to say "how d'ye do" and good-bye to the old students who had returned, up by Atlanta to get the first-honor man of my class to make an agent out of him, and off to the land of "water-millions," "cukes," and mosquitoes, and sand-flies again.

Albany is canvassed with equal success, the towns and cities of the "Land of Flowers" are invaded and stormed. Christmas has rolled round again, the year's work has been one of success; just thirty months have been spent as book agent ; twelve months before starting to college, two vacations, three months each, and the last twelve months making just thirty months, and eleven thousand dollars worth of Hitchcock's Analysis have been sold and delivered by this "special agent."

Thank God for success! Thank kind Providence for the generous spirit of the Southern man who stoops to help a college student in securing his education, though it be accomplished in the by-ways and hedges, talking over a book! Thank heaven for the sweet encouragement received at the hands of the noble women of this sunny land! Thanks to Rosa for her patience in my absence! Not a murmur nor complaint escaped her sweet lips while I struggled to accomplish the desires and purposes for which I left college. But six months remain now till graduation day, and then the matrimonial ties will bind us together.

Text-books are again resumed; the regular duties of a college life are met with renewed energy and ambition. How thankful should a heart be with whom heaven has dealt so kindly! A college course nearly completed ; not a dollar unpaid ; two little cottages in the "Gate City" rented out; some funds in the bank, and all made and saved from being a Special Agent!

A short note reaches me from the little village of L——. Indeed, it is the familar hand of Pauline Prestine! What's up?

"Mr. and Mrs. A. S. Prestine request your presence at the marriage of their daughter Pauline to Ernest Hastings, Tuesday evening, April —, 188 , at 8 o'clock. L——, Virginia."

If I had time I would go to see Pauline married; but business of a similar nature is soon to claim my attention, and an expected visit to the land of my youth will bring me into Pauline's presence time enough to wish her a long and happy life, any way. So, I just sent my compliments, with an orange blossom to twine in her brown hair on the eventful evening of her happily mated wedding.

Pauline had taken a trip from home, on the beautiful James, and had unexpectedly met her happy fate. Ernest Hastings was a gentleman of fine family, elegant home, and a prosperous mercantile business. He was intelligent, of noble disposition and very handsome. He was, indeed, such a character as Pauline had dreamed of, and she was equally attractive. Thus it was—a summer, an autumn, a winter—and spring brings the orange blossoms that twine her bridal wreath.

Well! well! A sheep-skin costs ten dollars, license one and a half dollars; which will bring the most happiness? Better buy both and secure all.

The rolling wheels of a two-horse phaeton go singing over the beautiful clay road, through the country, which leads to the residence on the hill, out from the Gate City. The "Special Agent" and the President of Emory College sit back in the softly-cushioned vehicle and listen to the songs of the mocking-bird as he carols his sweet notes on a bright summer day.

It is one o'clock p. m. Rosa and I stand at the hymenial altar. A few solemn words, some life-long vows, a few hurried good-byes, and off to our Blue Ridge home to spend the summer with loved ones among the grand old mountains that skirt the beautiful valley of Virginia.

"Well, Jack," said Pauline, as we met in the little village of L——, "if you and Rosa are as happy as Ernest and I are, long be your life, and strong be the ties that bind you together; to you two I give this *mountain laurel blossom*. When it fades, may *others* of a different character crown your happy brows.

Well, whether I shall spend my life in Georgia or Virginia, in the mountains or by the seashore, it will ever remain fresh in my memory, How I GOT MY EDUCATION!

Lovingly yours,
"THE SPECIAL AGENT."

THE END.

www.ingramcontent.com/pod-product-compliance
Lightning Source LLC
Chambersburg PA
CBHW030354170426
43202CB00010B/1369